MAY 0 7 '91   DATE DUE

Are
Mothers
Really
Necessary?

Are Mothers Really Necessary?

BOB MULLAN

WEIDENFELD & NICOLSON
New York

Published by Weidenfeld & Nicolson, New York
A Division of Wheatland Corporation
841 Broadway
New York, New York 10003-4793

Published in Canada by General Publishing Company, Ltd.

First published in Great Britain in 1987 by Boxtree Ltd.

Grateful acknowledgment is made to the following publishers for
permission to quote from the following works:

From *Contemporary Feminist Thought* by Hester Eisenstein. Copyright 1983
and reprinted with permission of G. K. Hall & Co., Boston.

From *The Art of Loving* by Erich Fromm. Copyright 1956 and reprinted
with permission of Harper & Row Publishers Inc., New York.

From *The Second Stage* by Betty Friedan. Published by Summit Books, a
Division of Simon & Schuster, Inc.

From *Attachment and Loss,* Volume I by John Bowlby. From *Attachment,*
Second Edition, by John Bowlby © Tavistock Institute of Human
Relations 1969, 1982. Reprinted by permission of Basic Books, Inc.,
Publishers, New York.

Library of Congress Cataloging-in-Publication Data
Mullan, Bob.
Are mothers really necessary? / Bob Mullan. — 1st ed.
p.   cm.
Bibliography: p.
Includes index.
ISBN 1-555-84237-2
1. Maternal deprivation.   2. Mother and child.   3. Bowlby, John.
I. Title.
BF723.M35M85   1988   88-9638
155.4′ 18—dc19   CIP

Manufactured in the United States of America

Designed by Irving Perkins Associates

First American Edition

10   9   8   7   6   5   4   3   2   1

Acknowledgments

A number of people offered help and encouragement to me in the researching and writing of this book. Peter Williams of TVS got the project off the ground in the first place, while Eileen Urwin and Garry Marvin helped with their secretarial skills. Most importantly, Anne Beech and Sarah Mahaffy of Boxtree demonstrated both faith and skill at the right times. In addition, I am grateful to the following for their kind permission to allow me to quote from their published works: Hester Eisenstein, *Contemporary Feminist Thought* (G. K. Hall); Erich Fromm, *The Art of Loving* (Harper & Row); Lloyd de Mause, *The History of Childhood* (Psychohistory Press); H. R. Schaffer, *Mothering* (Harvard University Press); Nancy Chodorow, *The Reproduction of Mothering* (University of California Press); Linda Pollock, *Forgotten Children* (Cambridge University Press); Betty Friedan, *The Second Stage* (Summit Books); John Bowlby, *Maternal Care and Mental Health* (World Health Organization) and *Attachment and Loss,* volume 1 (Basic Books); and John Bowlby, *Forty-four Juvenile Thieves* (Ballière, Tindall and Cox).

Contents

Preface

"Don't have a mother," he said. Not only had he no mother, but he had not the slightest desire to have one. He thought them very overrated persons. Wendy, however, felt at once she was in the presence of tragedy.

J. M. Barrie, *Peter Pan*

PETER Pan is not alone in devaluing mothers. Although we all know that our mothers are the central figures of our lives, especially when we are young, their work is not so highly rated or rewarded, either economically or in terms of status. Modern industrialized societies like our own consistently devalue mothers in many ways. For a start, contemporary attitudes hold that women who stay at home as full-time mothers are in some sense defective or unqualified to work outside the home, and are missing out on "real life." Moreover, social and individual problems are blamed on economic factors such as the level of unemployment, or on institutions such as education, which are held to be failing to instill law, order and morality in children. Childhood problems and faulty mothering are no longer central to such discussions.

This reluctance to give mothering its credit as the most

important work anyone can do, with the most profound consequences, is partly due to the fact that we *do* live in the age of rapidly changing expectations, social tensions, mass unemployment and dislocations. In addition, feminists have made everyone aware that women can and should engage in all forms of work outside the home. They have also, quite understandably, been eager to stop mothers from becoming scapegoats, held responsible for all society's ills. One way of doing this is to focus on other aspects of upbringing and society in general.

But such problems as divorce, the dissolution of families, violence, the experience of unemployment and the misery of loneliness are directly related to individual problems linked with childhood. *Are Mothers Really Necessary?* provides an alternative diagnosis and solution to some of these problems, through a revaluation of the child-parent relationship.

Childhood relationships, especially the central one with mother, are important because of their long-term consequences, but also because of the child's dependence and powerlessness in the relationship. Again the modern world does not seem to treat childhood with the sensitivity and respect it deserves. Children are often used as pawns in marital struggles, are dispensed with after separation or divorce, are subject to exploitation by advertising and are undervalued at home and at school. Most terribly, children seem to be sexually assaulted, abused and even murdered more than ever before.

Vincent Fontana, a leading writer on child abuse, believes we must redefine the notion of the "battered child." He argues that "any treatment by which the child's potential development is retarded or completely suppressed, by mental, emotional or physical suffering, is *mal*treatment, whether or not it is negative (as in deprivation of emotional or material needs) or positive (as in verbal abuse or battering)."[1] Distressing though it may be, it is worth reading what, in the extreme, we are capable of doing to our children, the same children we herald as representing the future. Fontana himself states that

the *battered-child syndrome* derived its descriptive name from the
nature of the child's injuries, which commonly include abra-
sions, bruises, lacerations, bites (human bites), haematoma,
brain injury, deep body injury (often with fractured ribs or
injuries to the liver or kidneys), "pulled" joints (often of the arm
or shoulder), combinations of fractures of the arms, legs, skull,
and ribs, burns and scalds, and marks left after strapping or
tying up. Roughly speaking, the injuries generally result from
knocking the child about, beating or whipping it with the
nearest object, throwing it around like a pillow—frequently
across the room—pulling and twisting an arm or leg, or
slamming the child on the floor or against a wall—literally battering it.[2]

He adds that the "ingenuity of parents" became better known
as time went by, and it was discovered that there was more to
battering than battery. Parents have inflicted almost every con-
ceivable type of injury on their children, using a vast array of
likely and unlikely weapons.

From the 1940s onwards, British psychiatrist John Bowlby
has both predicted such cases of human excess and has placed
the quality of mothering at the center of his diagnoses and
solutions for human problems. For Bowlby the consequences
of deprivation from mother and mothering can be both long-
lasting and dire. Separation from or loss of the mother, or a
poor relationship with the mother, is a sign of the danger to
come. As Bowlby says, life is about making and sustaining
meaningful relationships. In childhood we begin to feel confident with other people, liked and wanted—or we begin to feel
rejected, unwanted and out of place. To many feminists and
other critics, however, Bowlby exaggerated the importance of
the mother's role. His was a subtle form of "antifeminism," as
Margaret Mead put it. In *Are Mothers Really Necessary?*, I
intend to show that we need to heed Bowlby's arguments now
as never before. I will also show that some current feminist
thinking on motherhood enables us to enjoin Bowlby's argu-

ments with other theoretical positions—like feminism—which are usually held to be in opposition to his.

Like Bowlby, I do not romanticize motherhood. The inevitable financial strains of the family, the emotional changes that children bring, the sheer hard work, worry and anxiety, the lack of recognition and the endless daily loss of adult conversation—these make a romantic view untenable. But, discredited and out-of-date as they may seem to some, Bowlby's arguments can help us search for new ways to consider motherhood, and for new solutions to the problems of childhood, mothering and society.

Despite the fact that John Bowlby is British and has worked and lived in Britain all his life, it has been in the USA where *researchers* have seen the potential of his work and indeed much of American developmental psychology owes a debt to him. However, sadly neither in Britain nor in the USA has the societal implications of his work been acted upon. Yet both societies suffer from an unacceptable degree of child abuse and exploitation, let alone a high incidence of human misery. Similarly the roots to social problems like particular forms of crime and antisocial behavior are in childhood. To act upon Bowlby's insights would demand governmental and public intervention in order to provide a healthier context for "mothering" to be practiced. Like Britain the USA ignores Bowlby's arguments at its peril.

Are
Mothers
Really
Necessary?

1

"Expert" Advice

Historically, human societies have been pro-child; modern society is unique in that it is profoundly hostile to children. We in
the West do not refrain from childbirth because we are concerned about the population explosion or because we feel we
cannot afford children, but because we do not like children.

Germaine Greer, *Sex and Destiny*

IN arguing that there is a "profound lack of desire for children" in Western societies, Germaine Greer adds that "the
corollary is equally true, our children do not like us."[1] Almost
daily we can witness child suicides, and certainly there is much
unhappiness among children. Why should this be so? It is
because, I want to demonstrate, we do not value good mothering enough, and therefore do not practice it enough. An additional problem is that too much pressure is placed upon parents
to do the "right" things with their children, and indeed to
create the "perfect" child. What makes this worse, of course, is
that the mothers, *women,* usually have to listen to *male*
"experts" on the subject.

Dr. Spock is a case in point. In her study of Spock, Nancy
Weiss asserts that his *Baby and Child Care,* first published over
forty years ago, embodies a "world view" of rearing the young
"free from dissonance or conflict" or the recognition of "pov-

3

erty or cultural difference." Weiss concludes that such a world has "invented a motherhood that excludes the experience of many mothers."[2]

With Spock, as with other popular child psychology writers, it is extremely difficult to separate the content of what they say from the simple fact that they are *usually* men informing women of how to live their lives. This is a problem in that, to take the case of Spock, the advice is not *all* bad. For example, on working mothers Spock argues that "a few mothers, particularly those with professional training, feel that they must work because they wouldn't be happy otherwise. I wouldn't disagree if a mother felt strongly about it, provided she had an ideal arrangement for her children's care. After all, an unhappy mother can't bring up very happy children."[3]

On the other hand, and on the same subject of working mothers, Spock offers the following "advice":

> Some mothers *have* to work to make a living. Usually their children turn out all right, because some reasonably good arrangement is made for their care. But others grow up neglected and maladjusted. . . . Intelligent, well-adjusted citizens are the most valuable possessions a country has, and good mother care during early childhood is the surest way to produce them. It doesn't make sense to let mothers go to work making dresses or tapping typewriters in offices, and have them pay other people to do a poorer job in bringing up their children. . . . The important thing for a mother to realise is that the younger the child the more necessary it is for him to have a steady, loving person taking care of him. In most cases, the mother is the best one to give him this feeling of "belonging" safely and surely. She doesn't quit on the job, she doesn't turn against him, she isn't indifferent to him, she takes care of him always in the same familiar house.[4]

It is precisely this berating of women who work in offices "tapping typewriters" or mothers who make "dresses" that has, quite rightly, enraged many women over the past fifty years or so. Spock, for example, does not appear to realize that the mundane office and factory work he so derides is exactly the kind of work that his mothers had (and have) to undertake to "make a living."

Two Approaches

In an extensive and historical account of child-advice and child care "experts" entitled *Dream Babies,* Christina Hardyment suggests that such "experts" are distinguished from each other by their varied personalities, but that essentially, regardless of the time in which they are writing, they can be "classified as cuddly or astringent—lap theorists or iron men (or maidens)." She adds that the "latter claim that things are disgracefully lax, the former that fifty years ago child care was appallingly strict." Interestingly, Hardyment also notices how the very early "authorities" regularly anticipated most modern experts. For example, in 1767 George Armstrong, a pharmacist, wrote his *Account of the Diseases Most Incident to Children,* in which he stated that he disliked the idea of taking children away from their parents, and indeed himself "helped to make it unnecessary by opening a dispensary for the children of the infant poor, defraying most of its expenses from his own pocket." He treated thirty-five thousand children there, so that they had no need to go to children's hospitals. Armstrong anticipated Bowlby's own *Child Care and the Growth of Love* by two hundred years when he warned that "if you take a sick Child from its parent or Nurse, you break its Heart immediately."[5] Unfortunately, but not surprisingly, Armstrong lost his battle: his clinic was closed down after twelve years for lack of funds and sick children were again committed to the isolation of hospitals.

Another precursor of John Bowlby's was E. W. or Mrs. Bowditch, who, in her 1890 *Confidential Chats with Mothers on the Healthy Rearing of Children,* lamented

> the present fashion daily gaining ground of handing one's baby almost as soon as it is born into another's arms, often a total stranger's care. When only a month old, the little, soft, helpless mite, needing so greatly all the divine, instinctive love of a mother's heart, and all the tender shelter of a mother's arms, is, according to the approved system of the present day, ruthlessly turned over to the doubtful offices of a strange woman.

In subsequent chapters, I intend to concentrate on the "iron men" rather than the "lap theorists" because John Bowlby can clearly be seen as party to the latter position, but also because, whether we like it or not, the "iron man" tradition still influences us today. First, however, an overview of some leading experts is in order.

Mother's Milk

The tradition of "mothercraft" exemplified in the United States today by the La Leche League first held sway in the 1920s and 1930s in Britain due to the efforts of Truby King. Truby King was educated in Edinburgh and then moved to New Zealand, where he became superintendent of Seacliff Lunatic Asylum at Dunedin. At the asylum, which was well equipped with farms and gardens as occupational therapy for the patients, he was struck by the high death rate among bucket-fed calves from "scouring," a disease akin to gastroenteritis in babies. Subsequently he invented a "scientific system" of feeding, which in fact ended all deaths from this cause. He was convinced thereafter that a "human life a day could be saved if human mothers fed their babies in a similarly scientific and rational way."[6]

From 1907 onwards the Truby King movement started in earnest in New Zealand, where his theories were put into practice. Within five years the infant mortality rate there had dropped by a thousand a year. Truby King's "mothercraft movement" encouraged breast-feeding, guarded against over-feeding by rigid attention to the clock, taught a modified form of the complicated percentage feeding involving cow's milk and two Truby King patent additives, Kariel and Karilac, and instructed mothers in the orderly mothercraft that would produce a "Truby King baby." Such a baby is graphically described in *Mothercraft,* a handbook for mothers written by his adopted daughter Mary.

A real Truby King baby is completely breast-fed till the ninth month, and then slowly weaned onto humanised milk, with a gradual introduction to solid foods. . . . Truby King babies are fed four-hourly from birth, with few exceptions, and they do not have any night feeds. A Truby King baby has as much fresh air and sunshine as possible, and the right amount of sleep. His education begins from the very first week, good habits being established which remain all his life.

A Truby King baby is not too fat—every bit of his flesh is firm and clear, his eyes are bright and one only has to hold him for a moment to appreciate his muscular tone. He is not treated as a plaything, made to laugh and crow and "show off" to every visitor to please his parent's vanity; yet he is the happiest thing alive, gambolling with his natural playthings, his own hands and toes; he is interested in the new and wonderful things which come within the range of his vision and touch, and is as full of abounding vitality as the puppy playing in the yard.

He sleeps and kicks out of doors as much as the weather allows, and sleeps at night in the airiest bedroom, or on an open veranda or porch, being carefully protected by a screen to keep him from draughts. After he has gone through his regular morning performances of bathing and being "held out," and has had breakfast, he sleeps all morning. If he wakes a little before his 2 P.M. meal, all that one knows about it is a suddenly glimpsed chubby little leg or foot waved energetically from his cot for inspection, or a vigorous jerking of his pram.

Altogether, he is a joy from morning to night, to himself and to all the household—a perfectly happy and beautiful Truby King baby. The mother of such a baby is not over-worked or worried, simply because she knows that by following the laws of nature, combined with common sense, baby will not do otherwise than thrive.[7]

As Hardyment concludes, Truby King's "astonishingly idealised and simplified projection of babyhood still lives on as an ideal in many parents' minds, particularly for the grandmothers to whom the definition of a 'good' baby is one which prefers solitary confinement to human intercourse."[8]

J. B. Watson and Plastic Babies

Other advice writers claimed, at times, to base *their* ideas much more firmly in traditional research. One notable individual was the American J. B. Watson, the founder of "behaviorism"—a psychological theory of behavior which, essentially, views humans as Ping-Pong–playing pigeons with memories.

Like King, Watson believed the infant to be at the mercy of the parent. The baby's destiny was in the hands of its parents. Watson denied that the infant is born with any mental ability or predisposition. Watson's thinking followed that of the British philosopher John Locke, who propounded the view that the mind was a blank slate at birth—a tabula rasa. The extreme to which Watson was willing to carry this proposition is exemplified by his famous and often quoted statement:

Give me a dozen healthy infants, well-formed, and my own specified world to bring them up and I'll guarantee to take any one at random and train him to become any type of specialist I might select—doctor, lawyer, artist, merchant, chief, and yes, even beggarman and thief, regardless of his talents, penchants, tendencies, abilities, vocations, and race of his ancestors.[9]

Watson's "dream baby" was different from the ones desired by more modern child-centered advocates.

The happy child? A child who never cries unless actually stuck with a pin, illustratively speaking; who loses himself in work and play; who quickly learns to overcome the small difficulties in his environment without running to mother, father, nurse or some other adult; who builds up a wealth of habits that tides him over dark and rainy days; who puts on such habits of politeness and neatness and cleanness that adults are willing to be around him, at least part of the day; a child who is willing to be around adults without fighting incessantly for notice; who eats what is set before him and "asks no questions for conscience's sake"; who sleeps and rests when put to bed for sleep and rest; who puts away two-year-old habits when the third year has to be faced; who passes into adolescence so well-equipped that adolescence is just a stretch of fertile years, and who finally enters manhood so bulwarked that no adversity can quite overwhelm him.[10]

It is quite clear that such "opinions"—for that is merely what they are—can and do have an influence on mothers (and possibly fathers), especially first-time mothers who may be facing motherhood with trepidation and fear. For a start, the mother is mothering in an environment which includes the "cult of child psychology," the "explosion of books, pamphlets and magazine articles published in apparently ever-increasing numbers" as Cathy Urwin puts it,[11] which is mainly directed at first-time mothers and is concerned almost exclusively with infancy and the preschool years. Moreover, and despite endless examples to the contrary, ours is an environment in which "expertise" is valued—we are encouraged to let others do for us what we could well do for ourselves. Hugh Jolly, for example, in his *Book of Child Care: The Complete Guide for Today's Parents,* positively values his own role and asks that others share it with him.

> The modern mother takes for granted that she will have the advice of experts and will not have to rely on the advice of her mother. . . . This is not to belittle the enormous support which grandmothers can give. . . . But the modern mother is less convinced than her predecessors that her mother knows best.[12]

Ann Oakley may be exaggerating a little when she argues that "those who write the advice manuals see themselves as *waging war* on the influences women have over each other" (italics added).[13] But it is true, just to take the example of Jolly, that the advice writers seem to insist that modern mothers must stop listening to their mothers—or, for that matter, "to any woman who offers an opinion on motherhood, from the neighbour who starts solids early to a sister who warns that childbirth might actually *hurt.*"[14] This is a theme to which we will return.

To Bond or Not to Bond?

The notion of *bonding* (or, to be more precise, mother-infant interaction) is another aspect of mothering on which the "professionals" have been eager to offer opinions in the guise of expert advice, especially in recent years.

Maternal bonding, or mother-to-infant bonding, is of interest to us for three reasons. First, a discussion of it demonstrates that it is practically impossible to *prove* anything in this controversial area of mothering; second, it is quite inaccurately associated with Bowlby's work; finally, it has practical consequences if it is believed. It is an idea that men are propagating for the benefit of women who are clearly, in the proponents' minds, at any rate, unfamiliar with it. It is a very significant case of men's intrusion into women's lives as it concerns the period immediately following childbirth, a period when a woman could well be vulnerable to outsiders. At a time of privacy and intimacy, the bonding doctrine can be intrusive.

Much of the "evidence" which is used to support the bonding doctrine is derived from the study of premature babies and intensive care units. Researchers were interested in studying the relationship between the separation of babies from their mothers and their subsequent outcomes. Such separations were even seen by some researchers as being related to later outcomes like "failing to thrive" and indeed of child abuse. The high priests of such an approach are the American pediatricians Marshall Klaus and John Kennell, who claim that "mother disorders"—which for them range from mild anxiety to the "battered child syndrome"—invariably "result largely from separation and other unusual circumstances which occur in the early newborn period as a consequence of present hospital care policies."[15] Before looking at their ideas more closely, first a little history.

Martin Cooney, a pupil of P. Budin, the physician who published his famous book *The Nursling* in 1907, is extraordinarily significant in the history of the care of premature babies. His work shows how recent our general concern for infants really is.

Cooney exhibited his *Kinderbrutanstalt* ("child hatchery"), which specialized in caring for premature infants, at the Berlin Exposition of 1896; premature infants who were not expected to live were *given* to him by German physicians. He subsequently exhibited the infants in almost all the major fairs and expositions from 1902 until the New York World's Fair of

1940. The mothers of the infants concerned were not permitted to help take care of their offspring, although they were, as consolation, given free passes. Despite Cooney's sordid approach, many of his methods for the care of newborn children were adopted when premature nurseries were eventually established in the United States.

This is a long way from Klaus and Kennell's assertions concerning the importance of the "early newborn period." In their view, mothers should not only be available to the newborn, if medically possible, but actually, in a sense, be *omnipresent*. Responsibility for the baby's well-being lies with the mother. Klaus and Kennell base their arguments partly on developmental psychology and partly on the biological sciences. They argue that

> detailed studies of the amazing behavioural capacities of the normal neonate have shown that the infant sees, hears, and moves in rhythm to his mother's voice in the first minutes and hours of life, resulting in a beautiful linking of the reactions of the two and a synchronized 'dance' between the mother and the infant.[16]

The infant's appearance, and his broad array of sensory and motor abilities, evoke responses from the mother and provide several channels of communication that are essential in the bonding process and the initiation of a series of reciprocal interactions described above. In terms of the infant's abilities, for instance, Klaus and Kennell argue that merely six days after birth the infant can distinguish reliably by scent his mother's breast pad from the breast pad of other women. More biologically, they point to other levels of interaction:

> The infant's licking of the mother's nipple induces marked prolactin secretion and oxytocin release, which cause the uterus to contract thereby reducing postpartum bleeding. This early

interaction also permits the transfer of the mother's staph-
ylococcus and other bacteria to the infant so that it is colonized
with the mother's rather than the hospital's bacteria. Recent
discoveries in endocrinology, ethology, infant development,
immunology, and bacteriology have greatly increased knowledge of the reciprocal links at many levels between the parent
and infant. [17]

Such "facts" convince Klaus and Kennell of the importance
of bonding; for our purposes, it is salient to note three of the
seven principles involved:

1. There is a "sensitive period in the first minutes and hours of life
during which it is necessary that the mother and father have close
contact with their neonate for later development to be optimal."
2. During the process of the mother's bonding to her infant, it is
"necessary that the infant respond to the mother by some signal such
as body or eye movements." (In an extraordinary passage, Klaus and
Kennell add that they have sometimes described this, "You can't love
a dishrag.")
3. Some "early events have long-lasting effects. Anxieties about the
well-being of the baby with a temporary disorder in the first day may
result in long-lasting concerns that may cast long shadows and ad-
versely shape the development of the child."

I will be discussing the extent to which "bonding" can be
associated with Bowlby's work in the next chapter. Here, I
want to consider the difficulties of deciding what *proves* the
importance of bonding. Is it yet another case of male "special-
ists" dictating how mothers ought to behave?

Take the third "principle" of Klaus and Kennell's, namely the
long-lasting effects of first-day parental concern. How can
such an assertion be substantiated or proven? To support such
an assertion we have to rule out any later effects on the infant's
life that might counteract the experience of day one. In other
words, taking the example of the average woman's life span,

the remaining 25,500 days of her life cannot make up for her first experience. This possibility can only lead to *maternal guilt,* and yet it is an idea put forward among others by people who possess influence. Similarly, their first principle talks of a "sensitive period in the first minutes and hours of life" where optimal development should begin; surely this must vary in every case of childbirth, in every infant—some of whom may be sleepier than others—and surely we are talking about the early days, not minutes or hours.

A more measured claim is that of Judith Trowell in her study of Caesarian births, where the mothers appeared to have difficulties in initiating and developing relationships with their babies. As Trowell says, though, perhaps the mother has "missed the optimum" period for this to happen, even though such relationships can and do develop later. Trowell's conclusions are less rigid than Klaus and Kennell's and certainly more plausible.

> The implications of this for young women having a baby is striking. During labor, delivery, and the early postnatal days, new mothers (and fathers) pass through a period of emotional upheaval. At this time they are at their most open, most available emotionally, ready to embark on the new relationship. If this time is lost the relationship may be established more slowly and with more difficulty.[18]

Another quite depressing and guilt-inducing conclusion to emerge from the bonding doctrine, were it true—because we have seen already that Trowell for one does not adhere to it rigidly—would be that adoptive parents, who do not have the benefit of skin-to-skin contact with the newborn, could not hope to establish a proper relationship with their adopted children.

Returning to the implications of the bonding doctrine for mothers, the practice of the idea has tended to become doctrinaire.

The eminently sensible and humane idea of allowing a mother and her new baby to get to know one another by early, frequent and intimate social interaction becomes intrusive when the permissive "ought" of physical contact is replaced by an authoritarian "must." The mother *must* have physical contact with her infant (and presumably experience appropriate feelings) immediately after birth, otherwise something disastrous will happen, or—rather—not happen! She may not become bonded to her child.[19]

And as authors Wladyslaw Sluckin, Martin Herbert and Alice Sluckin continue to argue, it is no "ordinary relationship" referred to by the expression "normal bonding"; rather what is implied is a relationship of "unconditional love, self-sacrifice and nurturant attitudes which for the mother's part, will last a lifetime." Generally the authors conclude that, despite many studies, there is "little hard evidence" on the matter.

To complete the circle, and to demonstrate further the problem of "proof" in the area of mothering, P. Leiderman, in his review of the subject in 1981 which included his own investigations into mother-infant bonding, asserted that

even after the initial two to three months of separation from their premature infants, mothers do establish social bonds that cannot be differentiated from the bonds established by the mothers who initially were not separated from their infants . . . [that] . . . a sensitive phase, if it does exist, is at least three months in duration . . . [and that] . . . early contact does not necessarily facilitate social bonding; the data only suggest that this possibility exists for some individuals.[20]

Let us not forget, in any case, that it is extremely debatable whether or not hospitals in general, on both sides of the Atlantic, take much of an interest in the "bonding process." Certainly hospital birth generally does not lead to a high state of patient satisfaction; Sheila Kitzinger, for example, in a study of "bonding," noted that none of her first-time birth group who wished to have a home birth mentioned bonding as being important, but on the other hand all of the experienced mothers who had previous experience of a hospital birth referred to it. [21] What this might mean is that they considered hospital birth to be a negative experience, they felt their relationship with their baby was damaged by the experience or that they believed that "bonding" was important and that they had been denied this because of the experience of hospital confinement.

The discussion of bonding has demonstrated, I hope, that in considering mothering and the needs of children we are constantly confronted with problems of "proof" and that what we are dealing with are moral issues, with judgments and opinions. This is not in itself problematic once we are aware of it. The nearest we can possibly hope to come to both "proof" and "truth" are arguments that are narrow in scope and ambition and based on some concrete piece of data. Otherwise we simply have to choose those arguments that appeal both to our implicit sense of plausibility and our moral wishes.

In the South American Jungle with Stone Age Indians

A good example of the problem of "proof" is Jean Liedloff's arguments contained in her well-read *The Continuum Concept,* in which she advocates—for the first year of the infant's life at least—a closeness between the mother and infant through constant holding and carrying.

> From birth, continuum infants are taken everywhere. Before the umbilicus comes off, the infant's life is already full of action. He is asleep most of the time, but even as he sleeps he is becoming accustomed to the voices of the people, to the sounds of their activities, to the bumpings, jostlings and moves with-

out warning, to stops without warning, to lifts and pressures on various parts of his body as his caretaker shifts him about to accommodate her work or her comfort, and to the rhythms of day and night, the changes of texture and temperature on his skin and the safe, right feel of being held to a living body. His urgent need to be there would be noticeable to him only if he were removed from his place. His unequivocal expectation of these circumstances, and the fact that these and no other are his experience, simply carry on the continuum of his species.

Messages like this have a considerable impact, as is witnessed by the many people in the Western industrial nations who utilize all sorts of slings and harnesses. After spending over two years with "Stone Age Indians" in the South American jungle, Liedloff reevaluated the contemporary Western industrialized way of life and instead plumped for the Indian approach. In particular she believed that we had reneged on the principles of behavior of our species, Homo sapiens—principles established a long time ago.

Liedloff argues we were meant to behave quite differently from the way we currently do and that furthermore—and of course interrelatedly—we have constructed a world quite inappropriate to our "instincts." We consequently suffer from emotional deprivation, through all the cases of separation and lack of closeness that befall us.

They are the spelled-out, indisputable evidence, examples, proofs, for anyone who can doubt it, of the quintessential primacy of infant experience to the human personality. The extreme nature of their cases is but a magnifying glass through which one can see more clearly the deprivations and effects of the broader, more various and subtle range comprising normality. These "normal" deprivations are by now so tangled in the meshes of our cultures that they are almost entirely unremarked *except* at such extremes as manifest themselves in cost and danger to the rest of us (through violence, insanity, and crime, for example), and even then they are regarded without comprehension of any but the dimmest sort.[22]

However, if we lived in another manner—like her Stone Age Indians, the Yéquana—it would be altogether different. As she puts it, in the case of the infant kept in "constant contact with the body of a caretaker, his energy field becomes one with hers and excess energy can be discharged for both of them by her activities alone," with the result that the infant can "remain relaxed, free from accumulating tension, as his extra energy flows into hers." Not surprisingly Liedloff shares with Dr. Spock a concern about working mothers; she is sympathetic but at the same time extremely demanding.

> Many mothers have jobs to which they would not be permitted to bring their babies. But very often these jobs are a matter of choice, the mothers could, if they realized the urgency of their presence during the baby's first year, give up the job in order to avert the deprivations which would damage the baby's entire life and be a burden to her for years as well.
>
> On the other hand, there are mothers who must work. But they do not leave their children at home alone; they hire someone to look after them or leave them with a grandmother or make some other arrangement for the children to be accompanied. Whichever is the case, the caretaker can be instructed to carry the baby with her. Babysitters, hired for an evening, can be asked to sit the baby, not just the television set. They can hold the baby on their laps as they watch the television or do their homework. The noise and light will not disturb or harm him, but being alone will.
>
> Holding a baby while doing housework is a matter of practice. . . .[23]

How would we even begin to evaluate the arguments of Liedloff sensibly? Visit the Yéquana ourselves to test the validity of her arguments? How many would we have to meet and at what age? Should we construct human experiments in Yéquana methods of child-rearing?

In this chapter we have seen Dr. Benjamin Spock berating working mothers, J. B. Watson and Truby King claiming that a child's life is in the sole hands of her parents, Klaus and Kennell discussing their bonding doctrine, whereby both mother *and* infant have to attend to each other immediately after birth, and Jean Liedloff pointing to the need for constant closeness of the mother and infant in the first year especially, so that we can prevent a continuation of our current destructiveness. Which one is nearest to being right?

2

John Bowlby and Mothering

Mothers treat children differently from the way fathers do; they are complementary. There's a big overlap but there's a good deal of difference. The differences make perfectly good biological sense and to suppose that they are interchangeable is probably just wrong.

John Bowlby, "An Interview with John Bowlby
on the Origins and Reception of His Work"

JOHN Bowlby's belief in the importance of mothering, indeed the mother figure, has led to over thirty years of acrimonious debate and controversy. Feminists, for example, have asserted that his work is a subtle form of antifeminism, yet another attempt to keep women tied to the kitchen (and the child). Another criticism comes from the sociologists Susan Penfold and Gillian Walker, who argue that if too much emphasis is placed on an early mother-child relationship, mothers all too easily become the scapegoats of any failure, providing a convenient excuse for avoiding a critical examination of our social structures.[1] Psychologists on the other hand have argued that Bowlby's claims are too simple; they do not take into account the complexity of the child's life.

Bowlby's work is discussed in some detail here, because it is important to distinguish between what Bowlby actually

20

believes in and has said, which writings have been read and which ignored by his critics, and finally what other people think Bowlby has said.

John Bowlby left the University of Cambridge nearly sixty years ago, having completed his studies in preclinical medicine and with an interest in psychology. He then spent a year in a school for "maladjusted children," and this experience led him to explore relationships that developed in troubled families. Bowlby went on to complete his medical training at University College Hospital, London, his psychiatry training at the Maudsley Hospital, London, his psychoanalytic training at the Institute of Psycho-Analysis, London, and his training in child psychiatry at the London Child Guidance Training Centre. His training as a child psychoanalyst under the supervision of one of the pioneers in child analysis, Melanie Klein, was disrupted by the outbreak of the Second World War, during which he worked as an army psychiatrist. In this period, Bowlby published two papers, one of which was his membership paper for the British Psychoanalytical Society. The papers—"The Influence of Early Environment on the Development of Neurosis and Neurotic Character" and "Forty-four Juvenile Thieves"—were both published in the *International Journal of Psycho-Analysis* and contain the seeds of Bowlby's basic position on the pathogenetic effects of the disruption of family life.

Forty-four Juvenile Thieves: Their Characters and Home-life

Bowlby's study of the "forty-four thieves," published in book form in 1946, was carried out between 1936 and 1939 and consisted of an investigation of forty-four *consecutive* cases of children who attended a child guidance clinic and for whom "stealing was either a serious or a transitory system." This group of "thieves" was randomly selected for study, and only a minority of them had been charged in court. The children—boys and girls—ranged in age from five to sixteen years. Bowlby distinguished each child from the other through the concept of "character type," as shown in the table.

The "affectionless characters" particularly interested Bowlby. These children were distinguished from the others, according to him, by their remarkable lack of affection or warmth of feeling for anyone. One or two of the nine depressed children were unable to express "normal" affection during the depression, but this was, according to Bowlby, regarded as a change from their usual behavior. The "affectionless characters," on the other hand, had "apparently never since infancy shown normal affection to anyone and were consequently, conspicuously solitary, undemonstrative and unresponsive." Many of their parents and foster parents remarked that "nothing you said or did to them made any difference." The children responded neither to kindness nor to punishment.

"Nansi F." was nearly eight when first seen. Bowlby reports that her "schoolmistress complained that she was dishonest and pilfered money which was usually spent on sweets." This is from his description:

Character Type	Descriptions	Number
A. *"Normal"*	Children whose characters appear fairly normal and stable	2
B. *Depressed*	Children who have been unstable are now in a more or less depressed state of mind	9
C. *Circular*	Unstable children who show alternating depression and overactivity	2
D. *Hyperthymic*	Children who tend to constant overactivity	13
E. *Affectionless*	Children characterized by lack of normal affection, shame or sense of responsibility	14

Character Type	Descriptions	Number
F. *Schizoid*	Children who show marked schizoid or schizophrenic symptoms	4
Total		44

Different character types Bowlby found in his study of forty-four children who were known to steal.

Source: John Bowlby, *Forty-four Juvenile Thieves* (London: Ballière, Tindall & Cox, 1946), page 6.

History. She was the second of five children, all of whom lived with their widowed mother. They were looked after by a decrepit old grandmother because the mother had to work to make a living. The parents' marriage was described as having been "ideally happy. We never had a single quarrel or cross word, and when he died we were all broken-hearted." The father had been regarded as highly respectable. He died when Nansi was five. The mother also had a good reputation. Birth was normal and the child was bottle-fed like the other children. She appears to have thrived, and walked at ten months. At twelve months she fell ill with bronchitis and was in hospital for nine months altogether, having contracted pneumonia and measles whilst away. During all this time she never saw her parents, who were only permitted to visit her when she was asleep. On returning home she was frightened and very babyish and for some months she wetted and soiled her bed every night, although previously she had been clean.

Personality. The mother described the child as always having been the "odd one out." She never wanted to play with her sister or brothers and appeared to be quite indifferent to what happened to her and to how she was treated. When her younger brothers were born she treated it as if it did not concern her and showed no interest. If she wetted her knickers she never mentioned it and showed no shame if it was found out, but preserved her usual detached manner. If given Christmas or birthday presents she either lost them or gave them away. Her behaviour at school, from the accounts available, was not so unusual as at home. She was said to be a bright girl who enjoyed her work

and played about like any other child. But she was obviously
preoccupied with her faults, sometimes going spontaneously to
the teacher to say she had not been good all the week. . . .[2]

Bowlby observed variations in the behavior of the "affectionless children," yet despite these they had "so many traits in
common which distinguish them from the other thieves" that
he felt justified in grouping them together and regarding them
as "examples of a distinct clinical syndrome." When to the
similarity in their personalities is added the "discovery that
they have a remarkably distinctive early history—*prolonged
separations from their mothers or foster mothers*— . . . we have here
not only a distinct clinical syndrome, that of the affectionless
thief, but also an unusually clear example of the distorting
influence of a bad early environment upon the development of
personality" (author's italics).

Bowlby was writing in an era when the term (and event)
"broken home" was a factor believed to be particularly important in children and families with problems. For Bowlby the
term was sociological rather than psychological, and also
unhelpful. He was more interested in the specific and definable
element of the notion, and he believed rather that what was
important were situations in which the "child is *separated from
his mother or mother-substitute for long periods or permanently during
his first five years of life.*"[3] This idea was never to be absent from
Bowlby's later work; it is important to note here that Bowlby's
work in this period was concerned with studying the "deviant
and abnormal."

In the area of "delinquency" Bowlby reiterated this theme
for a number of years. In a paper, "Childhood Origins of
Recidivism," published in 1945 in *The Howard Journal*, he spe-
cifies the periods of separations he had observed as being
between six months and five years, and comments that Hitler's
well-known "Field-Marshal Goering appears to have suffered
in this way." In 1949, at a Royal Institution conference on the
"scientific study of juvenile delinquency," he argued that the

"individual who is mentally healthy is able to make mutually affectionate and lasting friendships with individuals and to cooperate satisfactorily with his neighbors," and that this capacity to make relationships is most "easily injured during its early development." Bowlby notes that the principal experiences of consequence in this connection are the continuity of the child's relation to his mother or mother substitute; the mother's total attitude towards him; and the particular procedures of handling, disciplining and training which she adopts.

> Children who either have no permanent mother figure or who are separated for long periods from their mothers, for instance by evacuation or prolonged hospitalisation, are apt to suffer from a severe inhibition of feelings of love. Such inhibition will lead to varying degrees of inhibition in the growth of conscience.[4]

The importance of the early years; the central role of the mother and how she behaves to her child in this relationship; the deleterious consequences for the child of maternal separation; and the importance of love were all constant themes in Bowlby's work.

Much of Bowlby's work at this time must be seen as progressive: his work and ideas developed against a criminological background of good and evil, of rigid deterministic biological ideas and of moralism. In a 1949 paper published in *The Magistrate,* Bowlby argues strongly against *punishment* and asserts that there is "no evidence whatsoever of the effectiveness of punishment." He suggests that punishment is ineffective as a means of reforming the persistent offender; in a century's time, such a punitive approach will be regarded as a curiosity. And once again, Bowlby points to the *causal* factor of early separation from the mother in criminal cases, and states that the "therapeutic" (as opposed to the legal) approach in these cases is intended to "unfreeze" the child's feelings: such therapy is based on the conviction that we all possess an urge to live on friendly terms with each other. He ends by conceding that his ideas could have a "revolutionary effect" and that it did not surprise him that his ideas "that the persistent delinquent needs help and kindness and not more punishment" met with resistance.

We could argue that his "kindness" somewhat misses the point, as it is the consequences and patterns of social structure that produce criminal acts, but the truth is to the contrary. Unemployment and poverty were no less visible in the 1940s than now; and not *all* human behavior can be explained in terms of social, economic, political or cultural factors. Clearly, the human personality is too complex a phenomenon to be reduced to this mechanistic level.

Maternal Care and Mental Health

It was the publication of *Maternal Care and Mental Health* in 1951, a report prepared on behalf of the World Health Organization as a contribution to the United Nations program for the welfare of homeless children, and most importantly the popular version of it, *Child Care and the Growth of Love* in 1953, which first brought Bowlby's name to a larger public.

In 1946 Bowlby had joined forces with James Robertson, a psychiatric social worker, and this partnership led to many studies of children who had been separated from their parents and were living either in residential nurseries or in hospitals. Robertson was studying the responses of children not only at the time of separation but, more importantly as it turned out, at the time of reunion. Nowadays, theorists interested in such matters value observations of a child's behavior upon reunion as an overriding criterion of the nature of her *attachment* to her mother.

Bowlby and Robertson argued, for example, that when a child of about eighteen to twenty-four months of age, who has previously had a normal relationship with her mother and has not previously been separated from her for more than a few hours, is separated from her and cared for in an impersonal environment, she commonly progresses through "three phases of emotional response which we describe as the phases of Protest, Despair and Denial."[5] In another paper—an explanation of one of James and Joyce Robertson's brilliant and moving films, *A Two Year Old Goes to Hospital*—the phases are explained in greater detail.

Laura, the subject of the film, is a child of two years and five months, with, in general, happy relations with both her parents. In emotional development she is advanced for her years. . . . Although her responses to the experience of separation contain much that we believe to be typical of the age span eighteen to thirty-six months, her expression of feeling is far more controlled than is usual. . . .

Among a child's responses after having been separated at this age the two commonest are: (1) an intense clinging to the mother, which can continue for weeks, months or years; and, (2) a rejection of the mother as a love object, which may be temporary or permanent. Her permanent rejection, though dramatic and extremely serious, is fortunately rare. . . . It is our experience that the great majority of children of about eighteen to thirty-six months respond to loss of their mothers, such as occurs when a child goes to a residential nursery or hospital, by protesting for the return of their mothers. Laura is no exception: as the film shows, she expresses her longing for her mother clearly, directly and very frequently, both in her remarks and her searching behavior. This phase of protest, however, never continues indefinitely: sooner or later, as despair grips the child, a new response gathers momentum—one of denying the need for the mother—a response in which repression is playing a large part. Laura never reaches this phase of complete denial; instead, her overt expression of wanting her mother continues actively throughout the eight days and, indeed, dominates her whole world.[6]

When the child returns home from these circumstances, there is also a characteristic sequence of responses; the form they take will depend both on the phase of separation response in which the child happens to be on her return, and on the insight with which she is handled. Robertson and Bowlby argue that it is probably "impossible for any adult really to imagine the intensity of feeling in a young child who has lost the care of his mother." Central to Robertson and Bowlby's work is the belief in stability (indeed, permanence) and certainty in relationships. In the case of hospital separations the child would learn by bitter experience that it is a mistake to become attached to any nurse, because nurses move on to other wards; thus, after a series of upsets at losing several nurses to whom she had given her trust and warm affection, she will gradually commit herself less and less to succeeding nurses and in time will stop altogether taking the risk of "investing love and dependence in anyone."[7]

Robertson's own research on the problems of young children in hospitals had a powerful impact on social policy in Britain, resulting in an increase in parental visiting time. For the child, going to hospital means leaving the care of his mother, and this is inevitably an "intensely unhappy experience for the small child—*no matter how kindly he is cared for by the doctors and nurses.*" An early hospitalization may "undo the effects of parents who have sought to protect their child from major upsets, knowing, as many parents now do, that emotional security in the early years is the basis of emotional security in later life."[8]

So it was, in the early 1950s, that the World Health Organization became interested in the many thousands of postwar refugees and asked Bowlby to write a report on the mental health of homeless children. During this period he visited the United States and many countries in Europe in the course of his research.

Maternal Deprivation

Early in his report Bowlby related the act of mothering to the state of mental health.

> What is believed to be essential for mental health is that the infant and young child should experience a warm, intimate, and continuous relationship with his mother (or permanent mother-substitute) in which both find satisfaction and enjoyment. . . . It is this complex, rich, and rewarding relationship with the mother in the early years, varied in countless ways by relations with the father and with siblings, that child psychiatrists and many others now believe to underlie the development of character and of mental health.[9]

When a child does not have this relationship she suffers *maternal deprivation*. This was meant by Bowlby, however, to be a *general* term, not just one applicable to homeless children. Thus, in Bowlby's model, a child is deprived, even though living at home, if her mother (or permanent mother-substitute) is unable to give her the "loving care small children need." Again, a child is deprived if for any reason she is removed from her mother's care.

This deprivation, according to Bowlby, will be relatively mild if he is looked after by someone whom he has already learned to know and trust, but may be considerable if the foster mother, "even though loving," is a stranger. All these arrangements, however, give the child "some satisfaction and are therefore examples of partial deprivation." They stand in contrast to the almost "complete deprivation" which is "still not uncommon in institutions, residential nurseries, and hospitals, where the child often has no one person who cares for him in a personal way and with whom he may feel secure."

The ill effects of such deprivation vary with its degree. Partial deprivation, which is less damaging than complete deprivation, can produce "acute anxiety, excessive need for love, powerful feelings of revenge, and, arising from these last, guilt and depression," while complete deprivation has "even more far-reaching effects on character development and may entirely cripple the capacity to make relationships."[10] It is important to note here that the report principally dealt with cases of complete deprivation, even though Bowlby then made comparisons with "normal" populations, a point critics later made.

The report did not deal in any detail with the matter of the child's relation to her father. For Bowlby, the reason for this relative omission was that all of the evidence in the area concerned the child's relation to her mother, which is, in ordinary circumstances, by far the most "important relationship during the early years." The mother cares for and comforts the child, whereas "in the young child's eyes father plays second fiddle."[11]

Bowlby points out that the evidence that the "deprivation of mother-love in early childhood can have a far-reaching effect on the mental health and personality development of human beings" comes from many sources, which fall into three main classes: direct observation of the development and mental health of children in institutions, hospitals and foster homes; retrospective studies of the early histories of adolescents or adults who have developed psychological illnesses; and follow-up studies of children who have suffered deprivations in their early years.

Bowlby summarizes the impressions that the studies make in total, arguing that although maternal deprivation always retards a child's development, as the direct studies show, often leading to physical and mental illness, the long-term effects of any such deprivation are not necessarily permanent. The retrospective and follow-up studies, however, suggest that there are few grounds for optimism. Some deprived children are clearly damaged for life.[12]

Such direct studies include, of course, Bowlby's own work with Robertson, but also numerous others including, for example, the work of René A. Spitz and Katherine M. Wolf on the hospitalization (and thus separation from mother) of infants. The "typical separated infant" of six to twelve months—listless, quiet, unhappy and unresponsive to a smile—was thought by Spitz and Wolf to be suffering from anaclitic depression, having many of the hallmarks of the typical adult depressive patient in a mental hospital. They describe the child's mood as one of "apprehension and sadness, there is a withdrawal from the environment amounting to rejection of it, there is no attempt to contact a stranger and no brightening if the stranger contacts him." Spitz and Wolf add that "activities are retarded and the child often sits or lies inert in a dazed stupor." Inability to sleep and loss of appetite lead to loss of weight and expose the child to recurrent infections.[13]

While discussing direct studies, Bowlby addresses the question of the specific age range of a child's vulnerability and concludes that "vulnerability diminishes slowly"; vulnerability between three and five years of age is still serious, though much less so than earlier. During this period children no longer live exclusively in the present, and can consequently conceive dimly of a time when their mothers will return, which is beyond the capacity of most children younger than three. Furthermore, the "ability to talk permits of simple explanations, and the child will take more readily to understanding substitutes."

Bowlby concludes that after "the age of five vulnerability diminishes still further, though there can be no reasonable doubt that a fair proportion of children between the ages of five and seven or eight are unable to adjust satisfactorily to separations, especially if they are sudden and there has been no preparation." While there is no reason to believe that all children under the age of three years, or a very large proportion of those between three and five, or a minority between five and eight invariably suffer through deprivation, Bowlby is interested in discovering why it is that some children suffer and others do not. After five, a happy and secure child can tolerate separation. An insecure child, however, can become pathologically anxious, misinterpreting the reasons for the separation as some form of punishment.

Bowlby's *Forty-four Juvenile Thieves* was an example of a retrospective study of deprivation, and he cites numerous cases of children who had (invariably) committed offenses and who were found to have "grossly disturbed emotional relationships with their mothers in their early years." Such children shared a number of features: superficial relationships; no real feelings; no capacity to care for people or to make true friends; an inaccessibility, exasperating to those trying to help; no normal emotional response; a curious lack of concern; deceit and evasion, often pointless; stealing; and lack of concentration at school.

Bowlby leant heavily on American psychiatrist W. Goldfarb's follow-up studies of children who were institutionalized in infancy,[14] and notes that the tenor of Goldfarb's summary of his findings on personality disturbances will by now be familiar to the reader.

> Briefly, the institution children present a history of aggressive, distractible, uncontrolled behaviour. Normal patterns of anxiety and self-inhibition are not developed. Human identifications are limited, and relationships are weak and easily broken. . . . Finally, the fact that the personality distortions caused by early deprivation are not overcome by later community and family experience must be stressed. There is a continuity of essential traits as late as adolescence. If anything, there is a growing inaccessibility to change.[15]

Very importantly, Bowlby emphasized a serious shortcoming in Goldfarb's discussion—"namely, his tendency to imply that all institutions and their products are the same."

In summarizing his "evidence," Bowlby asserts that "the evidence is now such that it leaves no room for doubt regarding the general proposition" that the "prolonged deprivation of the young child of maternal care may have grave and far-reaching

effects on his character and so on the whole of his future life."
Controversially he adds that "although it is a proposition
exactly similar in form to those regarding the evil after-effects
of rubella in foetal life or deprivation of vitamin D in infancy,
there is a curious resistance to accepting it." In a statement that
was to be oft-repeated by his critics over the following
decades, Bowlby adds:

> It is now demonstrated that maternal care in infancy and early
> childhood is essential for mental health. This is a discovery
> comparable in magnitude to that of the role of vitamins in
> physical health, and of far reaching significance for pro-
> grammes of preventive mental hygiene.[16]

In a discussion on the mother–infant relationship, Bowlby
repeats the point that in this "warm, intimate and continuous
relationship" both partners need to find both satisfaction and
enjoyment—"it is [the] live human relationship which alters
the characters of both human partners." As Bowlby puts it,
the "provision of a proper diet calls for more than calories and
vitamins: we need to enjoy our food if it is to do us good." In
the same way, the "provision of mothering cannot be considered in terms of hours per day but only in terms of the enjoyment of each other's company which mother and child
obtain." For Bowlby such enjoyment and close identification
of feeling is only possible for either party if the relationship is
continuous—both parties need to experience a sense of
belonging, from which they derive satisfaction and which
enables them to make a further commitment.[17] He adds, in
another historic passage, that the "provision of constant attention day and night, seven days a week and 365 in the year, is
possible only for a woman who derives profound satisfaction
from seeing her child grow from babyhood, through the many
phases of childhood, to become an independent man or
woman, and knows that it is her care which has made this
possible."[18]

This intensity leads Bowlby to argue that this mother love is easily provided within a family, with the exception of the very worst cases, and that it is very difficult to provide outside it. [19]

Even bad parents, according to Bowlby, can offer much to a child in terms of continuity of care, giving that child an invaluable sense that there is at least someone to whom she is important and for whom she has value. This led Bowlby to another controversial conclusion, one that affected subsequent child care (and social work) policy and was once more the target of later criticism. According to Bowlby, it is against this background that "the reason why children thrive better in bad homes than in good institutions and why children with bad parents are, apparently unreasonably, so attached to them can be understood."[20]

Bowlby qualifies his claim by adding that "the evidence . . . that bad homes are often better than good institutions—is far from definitive and in any case all depends on how bad is the home and how good the institution," but he adds that no home at all is probably worse than a bad one.

Bowlby explains this by suggesting that, say, despite much neglect, either parent has almost always and in countless ways been kind to the child from the day of his birth onwards; however much the outsider sees to criticize, the child "sees much to be grateful for—at least his parents have cared for him after a fashion all his life, and not until someone else has shown herself to be equally or more dependable" has the child a reason to trust that person. Quite realistically, even by today's standards, Bowlby adds that the most devoted foster parents can never experience—or show—the same sense of total obligation to the child that even the worst of parents possess. "Even for good foster-home agencies the rate of replacement is deplorably high; even in good institutions the turnover of staff is a constant problem."[21]

In *Maternal Care and Mental Health*, Bowlby then moves onto three interrelated circumstances in which a child suffers mater-

nal deprivation: the partial deprivation of living with a mother
or permanent mother substitute, including a relative, whose
attitude towards her is unfavorable; the complete deprivation
of losing her mother (or permanent mother substitute) by
death, illness or desertion and having no familiar relatives to
care for her; the complete deprivation of being removed from
her mother (or permanent mother substitute) to strangers by
medical or social agencies. He points out that his report concentrates on the grosser forms of deprivation and the possible
prevention of these, and as the great majority of them are the
result of "family failure" he will therefore focus on cases
where a child never had a family, where her family had broken
down or where social agencies had removed her from her home
because it had been judged to have failed.

Bowlby divides those natural home groups that have failed
to care for the child into three categories:[22]

1. Natural home group never established:
   Illegitimacy

2. Natural home group intact but not functioning effectively:
   Economic conditions leading to unemployment of bread-winner
   with consequent poverty
   Chronic illness or incapacity of parent
   Instability or psychopathy of parent

3. Natural home group broken up and therefore not functioning:
   Social calamity—war, famine
   Death of a parent
   Illness requiring hospitalization of a parent
   Imprisonment of a parent
   Desertion by one or both parents
   Separation or divorce
   Employment of father elsewhere
   Full-time employment of mother

Any family suffering from one of these conditions—and
note that one is the "full-time employment of mother"—must,

according to Bowlby, be regarded as a *potential* source of deprived children. Whether or not these children actually become deprived will depend on whether both parents or only one is affected; whether, if only one parent is affected, help is given to the other; and whether relatives or neighbors are able and willing to act as substitutes. Not surprisingly, given both his belief in the efficacy of the family and the reality of trying to raise children on one's own, Bowlby argues that there is "no group of children in danger of deprivation in whose production psychiatric factors play a larger part than illegitimates"; this is the first point in the *cycle of deprivation* mentioned in his work. Bowlby elaborates this controversial point when he somewhat naïvely evaluates the social and economic trends of the time and concludes that relative social and economic deprivation create a self-perpetuating cycle of instability and deprivation, passing from one generation to the next.[23]

In his arguments for the prevention of such "family failures" and possible subsequent *social* cycles of deprivation, he argues for both direct aid to families and long-term community programs. He makes claims for direct *socioeconomic* aid—"on grounds of financial economy as well as the child's mental health, then it is to be hoped that governments and voluntary agencies alike will, before allocating further funds for the care of children away from their homes, consider whether everything possible has been done financially to assist parents to care for them at home"—and also *sociomedical* aid, as socioeconomic aid is "often useless unless help of a sociomedical aid is given as well." He adds that in many cases there would be "no economic problem at all were it not for the physical or mental illness, psychopathic character, or conflict in the home." Among his suggestions there is the development of marriage guidance, for example, and the provision of "rest homes" to which mothers may go with their children.

It is often conveniently forgotten that Bowlby also advocates long-term community programs, and in terms of socioeconomic developments he observes that we should never forget the great economic vulnerability of the family with children.[24] As Beveridge reported, in England "a family still remains the greatest single cause of poverty," a condition which also holds true elsewhere in the world. On the subject of family allowances in England Bowlby argues that they were a "vital step in the right direction" even though it must be "considered whether some specially increased provision should not be made for children under five or three."

He also advanced long-term programs of a sociomedical nature, and in particular programs of psychotherapy and psychiatric social work. Again he believes that such programs will be of particular help in breaking the cycle that produces illegitimate children. However, for the mother of an illegitimate child who cannot be helped (if need be) he advocates early adoption, in fact very soon after birth— "it may tentatively be inferred that in skilled hands adoption can give a child nearly as good a chance of a happy home life as that of the child brought up in his own home."[25]

Bowlby concludes *Maternal Care and Mental Health* by reasserting that "mother love in infancy and childhood is as important for mental health as are vitamins and proteins for physical health." He develops his biological theme and pronounces that

> the proper care of children deprived of a normal home life can now be seen to be not merely an act of common humanity, but to be essential for the mental and social welfare of a community. For, when their care is neglected, as happens in every country of the Western world today, they grow up to reproduce themselves. Deprived children, whether in their own homes or out of them, are a source of social infection as real and serious as are the carriers of diphtheria and typhoid. And just as preventive measures have reduced these diseases to negligible proportions, so can determined action greatly reduce the number of deprived children in our midst and the growth of adults liable to produce more of them.[26]

Bowlby remained pessimistic about *therapeutic change* for deprived children—"the evidence available suggests that nothing but prolonged residence with an adult, with insight into the problem, skill in handling it, and unlimited time to devote to her charge, is likely to be of much avail," and that this is "not only very expensive but could never be made available to more than a tiny fraction of cases." Again prevention is better than cure.

The popularized version of the report, published as *Child Care and the Growth of Love* in 1953, was a best seller and guaranteed that the report's findings, arguments and proposals reached a wide audience. The book became a manual for the social work professions as well as certain schools of child psychiatry.

Before proceeding, it is worth summarizing the main points of *Maternal Care and Mental Health*—that mothering (by the natural mother or mother substitute) is a two-way process, characterized by love, responsiveness and continuity; that fathers usually play a supportive role to the central mother-child relationship; that the family facilitates the proper performance of this mother-child relationship; that separations and hence disruptions of the mother-child relationship can lead to mental ill health, which can also occur when such relationships fail to develop in the first place (through separations); that deprived children as parents tend to reproduce the circumstances which led to their own deprivations; that damaged children are difficult to help, and that adverse effects can last a long time and in some cases are effectively irreversible; and that bad homes are invariably preferable to good institutions for commitment exists in the homes, the child trusts the parent (however misplaced that trust may be), and both foster care and institutional care cannot provide the necessary quality and consistent mothering required for good mental health.

Although *Maternal Care and Mental Health* was concerned with the study of deprivations both partial and complete, and despite the fact that the report was a study of *abnormal* relationships, the report was the centerpiece of Bowlby's intellectual development, which moved him from studies of maladjustment and delinquency in children to the studies of separation, which then led to a consideration of that which had been disrupted—namely, the "ordinary" home conditions we tend to take for granted but which are essential to mental and physical well-being.

Can I Leave My Baby?

Although not known as a proselytizer, Bowlby reiterated his themes in a number of popular outlets other than *Child Care and the Growth of Love*. In *The Roots of Parenthood*, written for the National Children's Home, for example, he repeats his claim about the social-cyclical nature of deprivation.

> The roots of parenthood lie in the child's relations to his own parents in his earliest years. The love which a mother has for her children is a reflection of the love which she received when she was a little girl. The love which a father has for his children is a reflection of the love which he received when he was a little boy. It is in childhood that we learn to love. To some this proposition seems so obvious that it is hardly worth dwelling on. To others it seems so revolutionary as to be ridiculous. [27]

In *Can I Leave My Baby?*, published for the National Association for Mental Health, he repeated his claim that the central role anyone can play in human life is that of mothering (especially of the small child) and gave a qualified "yes" to the question posed by the title.

> A mother's job is inevitably exacting, especially when her children are small. It is a craftsman's job and perhaps the most

skilled in the world. But what worthwhile job is not exacting? And the very fact that a mother's role is so essential and worthwhile is largely responsible for the satisfaction which most mothers find in their families. They may be dog-tired and consider themselves shorter-tempered than they could wish, but it is a great compensation to feel that they *really matter,* that no one else will do. . . .

Mothers sometimes ask: then can we *never* leave our small children? I do not believe that anyone has ever suggested that they should not. It is an excellent plan to accustom babies and small children to being cared for now and then by someone else—father, for instance, or granny or some other relation or neighbour.[28]

This stringency is more pronounced when it comes to the working mother, where Bowlby says that "leaving a small child whilst you go out to work needs much more care." If the child's maternal grandmother is nearby or a dependable neighbor is available, "it may work out all right," but it does "need regularity, and it must be the same *woman* who cares for him" (italics added).[29]

Significantly, in this same pamphlet Bowlby uses "evidence" from the social life of other animals to support his arguments. For example, he discusses the need for "companionship" in "young creatures"—"whether it is a brood of ducklings in a pond, twin lambs in a meadow, or a human toddler around the house, the young are quickly distressed if they get lost and scamper to get close to their mothers as soon as anything happens which frightens them." He concludes that there seems "little doubt that this tendency of young animals to attach themselves closely to their parents is a primary 'instinct'—as primary as the 'instincts' to feed and to avoid pain. This is hardly surprising when we come to consider it, since it is plain that in a state of nature the young animal would fare very badly if he were to become isolated from his parents. Human young are no exceptions."[30] This line of reasoning was particularly important for the future direction of Bowlby's work. It proved to be the key which enabled him to relate his work on separation and abnormal families to normal human processes. To understand this we have to backtrack a few years.

Bowlby believed both prior to and certainly at the time of writing *Maternal Care and Mental Health* that the first task he had to grapple with if he was to develop a theory of the mother-child relationship from his observations of cases of separation was to "understand the nature of the child's tie to his mother." Like Paul on the road to Damascus, Bowlby too was blinded by enlightenment, but in his case the light came from ethology.

> During the summer of 1951 a friend had mentioned to me the work of Lorenz on the following responses of ducklings and goslings, and this leads me to ethology. Here, I found a new world, one in which scientists of high calibre were investigating in non-human species many of the problems with which I was grappling in the human, in particular the relatively enduring relationships that develop in many species, first between young and parents, and later between mated pairs, and some of the ways in which these developments can go awry. . . . Amongst other things, their work showed that in some animal species a strong bond to an individual mother-figure could develop without the intermediary of food, that it could develop rapidly during a sensitive phase in early life, and that it tended to endure. This provided an alternative model for consideration and one that had a number of features which seemed possibly to fit the human case. From that moment I was on a new track.[31]

Attachment

Put simply, Konrad Lorenz demonstrated that chicks, ducklings and goslings exposed to a moving object during a sensitive period soon after hatching will learn to follow it, responding to it as they would to their own parents. After relatively little experience with one object, their responsiveness becomes more or less limited to it. For example, when hatched in an incubator and shown any moving object, even a matchbox or a large balloon, they will follow this, and will later continue to do so even when faced with a choice between the object and their own parents. Bowlby himself summarized the generic use of the term "attachment," and argues that the term always implies the development of a clearly defined preference, a preference that develops fairly quickly, and usually during a limited phase of the life cycle, and a preference that, once formed, remains comparatively fixed.

In the first volume of his trilogy on the processes of attachment, separation and loss—*Attachment and Loss*. Volume 1: *Attachment*—Bowlby argues that the development of attachment behavior in human infants, though much slower, is "of a piece with that seen in non-human mammals." He summarizes the development of attachment behavior in humans in the following way:[32]

1. In human infants social responses of every kind are first elicited by a wide array of stimuli and are later elicited by a much narrower array, confined after some months to stimuli arising from one or a few particular individuals.

2. There is evidence of a marked bias to respond socially to certain kinds of stimuli more than to others.

3. The more experience of social interaction an infant has with a person the stronger his attachment to that person becomes.

4. The fact that learning to discriminate different faces commonly follows periods of attentive staring and listening suggests that exposure learning may be playing a part.

5. In most infants attachment behaviour to a preferred figure develops during the first year of life. It seems probable that there is a sensitive period in that year during which attachment behaviour develops more readily.

6. It is unlikely that any sensitive phase begins before about six weeks and it may be some weeks later.

7. After about six months, and more markedly so after eight to nine months, babies are more likely to respond to strange figures with fear responses, and more likely also to respond to them with strong fear responses, than they are when they are younger. Because of the growing frequency and strength of such fear responses, the development of attachment to a new figure becomes increasingly difficult towards the end of the first year and subsequently.

8. Once a child has become strongly attached to a particular figure, he tends to prefer that figure to all others, and such preference tends to persist despite separation.

In other words, according to Bowlby, the way in which attachment behavior develops in the human infant and becomes focused on a discriminated figure is sufficiently like the way in which it develops in other mammals, and in birds, for it to be included, legitimately, under the heading of *imprinting,* as generically used.

In discussing the role of attachment behavior in nature— cows and calves, mares and foals, ewes and lambs—Bowlby asks why these animals remain in each other's company, and what is achieved by their doing so? Bowlby's answer is that such behavior maintains proximity to another animal and restores it when it has been impaired, and ultimately is useful as something of survival value, as protection against predators. In relating such evidence to human infants Bowlby argues that there is good evidence that in a family setting most infants of about three months are already responding differently to mother as compared with other people. When she sees her mother, an infant of this age will smile and vocalize more readily and follow her with her eyes for longer than she does when she sees anyone else. But not only does the infant recognize her mother, she also behaves in a way that maintains her proximity to her, and such proximity-maintaining behavior is seen at its most obvious when mother leaves the room and the infant cries, or cries and also attempts to follow her.

Bowlby suggests that

> whilst readiness to develop attachment is low in the weeks after birth, it increases during the second and third months. The fact that by the end of a half-year the elements of attachment behaviour are clearly established in many infants suggests that during the preceding months—fourth, fifth and sixth—most infants are in a high state of sensitivity for developing attachment behaviour.
>
> Beyond a general statement of this kind it is not possible to go. In particular, there is no evidence whether sensitivity is greater during any one of these months than during another.[33]

It is certain, however, he adds, that after the age of about six months, conditions for developing attachment tend to become more complicated.

Bowlby argues that attachment behavior is exhibited strongly and regularly in most children almost until the end of the third year. Then a change occurs, and after their third birthday most children become increasingly able in a strange place to feel secure with subordinate attachment figures, although such a feeling of security is conditional. The subordinate figures must be familiar to the child. The child should be in a calm and healthy state—and should know his mother's whereabouts and be assured that he can reestablish contact with her at very short notice. If these conditions do not apply, the child's behavior is likely to become disturbed.

For Bowlby, no form of behavior is accompanied by stronger feelings than attachment behavior—the figures towards whom it is directed are loved and their advent is greeted with joy. So long as a child is in the unchallenged presence of a principal attachment figure, or within easy reach, she feels secure. A threat of loss creates anxiety, and actual loss, sorrow; both are likely to arouse anger.

Who Is the Principal Attachment Figure?

Whom the child selects as her principal attachment figure, and moreover to how many other figures she becomes attached, depends in large part on who cares for her and on the composition of the household in which she is living. The people in question are most likely to be her natural mother, father, older siblings and perhaps grandparents, and it is from among these figures that a child is most likely to select both her principal attachment figure and her subsidiary attachment figures.

Although it is usual for a child's natural mother to be her principal attachment figure, Bowlby argues that the role can be taken effectively by others. As long as a mother substitute behaves in an appropriately mothering way towards a child, the child will respond in the same way as another child would treat her natural mother. For Bowlby what comprises a "mothering way" of treating a child is for the adult to engage in "lively social interaction" with her, and to respond readily to her "signals and approaches." However, Bowlby adds that it is undoubtedly more difficult for a substitute mother to behave in a completely mothering way towards a child than it is for a natural mother.

For example, knowledge of what elicits mothering behaviour in other species suggests that hormonal levels following parturition and stimuli emanating from the newborn baby himself may also be of great importance. If this is so for human mothers also, a substitute mother must be at a disadvantage compared with a natural mother. On the one hand, a substitute cannot be exposed to the same hormonal levels as the mother; on the other, a substitute may have little or nothing to do with the baby to be mothered until he is weeks or months old. In consequence of both these limitations, a substitute's mothering responses may well be less strong and less consistently elicited than those of a natural mother.

It is a mistake, according to Bowlby, to suppose that a young child diffuses her attachment over many figures in such a way that she gets along with no strong attachment to anyone, and consequently without missing a particular person when that person is away. On the contrary, there is a strong bias for attachment behavior to become directed mainly towards one particular person. Bowlby believes this to be so important as to merit a special term, "monotropy."

Bowlby describes three main patterns of attachment: securely attached to the mother; anxiously attached to mother and avoidant; and anxiously attached to mother and resistant. A main characteristic of infants classified as securely attached to mother is that they are active in play and also in seeking contact when distressed after a brief separation, they are readily comforted and soon return to absorbed play. Infants classified as anxiously attached to mother and avoidant (approximately 20 percent of most samples of researched children) avoid her during reunion. Many of them treat a stranger in a more friendly manner than their own mother. Infants classified as anxiously attached and resistant (approximately 10 percent in most samples of researched children) oscillate between seeking proximity and contact and resisting interaction. Some are markedly more angry than others; a few, more passive.

Why the variation? In an important passage Bowlby partly answers the question by saying that "it is evident that the particular pattern taken by any one child's attachment behaviour turns partly on the initial biases that the infant and the mother each bring to their partnership and partly on the way that each affects the other during the course of it."[34] Importantly Bowlby argues that by the time the "first birthday is reached both mother and infant have commonly made so many adjustments in response to one another that the resulting pattern of interaction has already become highly characteristic." However, he adds that these patterns of interaction can be affected by changes such as illness, separation, the arrival of a new child and so on, which can so alter the behavior of either mother or child that the relationship between them is radically changed, for the worse. It is important to distinguish an attachment to someone from attachment behavior; to say that a child is attached or has an attachment to someone means that she is strongly disposed to seek proximity and contact with a specific figure and does so in certain situations, notably when she is "frightened, tired, or ill." Attachment behavior, by contrast, refers to any of the "various forms of behaviour that a child commonly engages in to attain and/or maintain a desired proximity." Bowlby's theory of attachment is an attempt to explain both attachment behavior with its episodic appearance and disappearance, and also the enduring attachments that children and older individuals make to particular figures. That attachment behavior in adult life is a straightforward continuation of attachment behavior in childhood is shown, according to Bowlby, by the circumstances that lead an adult's attachment behavior to become more readily elicited—"in sickness and calamity, adults often become demanding of others; in conditions of sudden danger or disaster a person will almost certainly seek proximity to another known and trusted person." In such circumstances an increase of attachment behavior is recognized by all as natural. And as Bowlby adds, "To dub attachment behaviour in adult life regressive is indeed to overlook the vital role it plays in the life of man from the cradle to the grave."[35]

This final point is important for two reasons. First, it shows that Bowlby believes he has produced a theory which can help us to understand the long-term consequences of our early childhood experiences. Secondly, it pinpoints another important aspect of Bowlby's theory of attachment, an aspect which is the linchpin between early life and later adulthood: our attachment experiences and attachment histories produce for us internal working models of both the world outside us (including the principal attachment figure and others) and of ourselves. Bowlby summarizes the importance of such models:

> From the early months onwards and throughout life the actual presence or absence of an attachment figure is a major variable that determines whether a person is or is not alarmed by any potentially alarming situation; from about the same age . . . a second major variable is a person's confidence, or lack of confidence, that an attachment figure not actually present will none the less be available. . . . The younger the individual the more influential is the first variable, actual presence or absence; up to about the third birthday it is the dominant variable. After the third birthday forecasts of availability or unavailability become of increasing importance, and after puberty are likely in their turn to become the dominant variable.[36]

These models are useful in approaching and guiding behavior in new situations. For example, according to the attachment theorist Inge Bretherton, if the child's experience had led her to construct a model of the attachment figure as a person likely to provide support when needed, "close monitoring of the figure's whereabouts may be less necessary."[37]

These internal working models of attachment figures and self, once organized, tend to operate outside conscious awareness. For this reason, and because new information is assimilated to existing models, the models tend to be resistant to dramatic change.

Bowlby outlines what he considers to be the development of personality along the lines proposed by attachment theory in the following manner:

> A young child's experience of an encouraging, supportive and cooperative mother, and a little later father, gives him a sense of

worth, a belief in the helpfulness of others, and a favourable model on which to build future relationships. Furthermore, by enabling him to explore his environment with confidence and to deal with it effectively, such experience also promotes his sense of competence. . . . Thereafter on how someone's personality has come to be structured turns his way of responding to subsequent adverse events, among which rejections, separations and losses are some of the most important.[38]

Separation and Loss

Bowlby's further two volumes of his trilogy—*Separation* and *Loss*—devote themselves to numerous descriptions of separations and losses that cause disruptions of attachments or the failure to make attachments in the first place. We have already seen that in Bowlby's earlier work this was exactly his focus— the study of when mothering goes wrong, especially as reviewed in *Maternal Care and Mental Health*. In these later volumes the presence or absence of a mother figure is the key variable. In this connection Bowlby draws two conclusions.[39]

1. The sequence of *intense* protest, followed by despair and detachment, which first caught our attention, is due to a combination of factors, of which the kernel is the conjunction of strange people, strange events, and an absence of mothering either from mother herself or from a capable substitute.

2. Because separation from mother figure even in the absence of these factors still leads to sadness, anger, and subsequent anxiety in children aged two years and over, and to comparable though less differentiated stress responses in younger ones, separation from mother figure is in itself a key variable in determining a child's emotional state and behaviour.

However, Bowlby also makes the point that since "distress at being separated unwillingly from an attachment figure is an indissoluble part of being attached to someone," changes occurring with age, in the form of response to separation, accompany "changes in the form that attachment behaviour takes." As far as attachments to loved figures are an integral part of our lives, so also is the capacity to feel distress on separation from them and anxiety at the prospect of separation.[40]

Unlike the evidence cited in *Maternal Care and Mental Health*, in these later volumes Bowlby utilizes studies of the young of other species in addition to the responses of human young. Of particular importance was the work of the ethologist Harlow and his colleagues. Bowlby in no way suggests that the early development of the mother-baby relationship in humans is just like the parent-offspring relationships in other species. Bowlby makes use of aspects of such relationships common to a wide range of species, and suggests that they are likely to be important in humankind also.

In his original experiments, Harlow reared two groups of monkeys on inanimate surrogate mothers, both made from wire, but one covered with terry cloth. Half the babies received milk from a bottle on the wire mother, and half from the cloth mother. Regardless of which "mother" was providing the food, all the infants spent most of their time on the cloth mother. Later, in unfamiliar situations, the cloth mother apparently gave some reassurance and security, but the wire mother none.[41] Muriel Beadle noted that the babies used the cloth mother as a psychologically reassuring "home base."[42] If the cloth mother was removed, leaving only the wire mother, the infant monkeys "ran across the test room, threw themselves down on the floor, clutched their heads and bodies and screamed in distress." This was seen as evidence that bodily contact is the single most important requirement in the formation of an infant's attachment to its mother. Bowlby incorporated the element of warmth into his requirements for a satisfying mother-baby relationship, but most importantly the significance of bodily contact helped Bowlby formulate the fundamental notion that "attachment behaviour is conceived as distinct from feeding behaviour and sexual behaviour and of at least equal significance in human life."[43]

In the third volume of the trilogy, *Loss,* Bowlby interprets more dramatically the evidence which formed part of his discussion of separation in his earlier works. Bowlby begins by repeating the original data on the child's response to separation from the mother figure, in the cycle from protest to despair as the child's belief that her mother will return begins to fade leaving her in a state of "unutterable misery." Bowlby then adds that although this behavior must have been known for centuries, it is only in recent years that it has been "described in the psychological literature and called by its right name— grief."[44]

Another important argument that appeared in the earlier work, especially the WHO report, namely that of the *social* cyclical nature of deprivation, reappears in the volume on separation. Bowlby argues that because children tend "unwittingly to identify with parents" and therefore, when they become parents, to adopt the same patterns of behavior towards their children that they themselves experienced during their own childhood, patterns of interaction are transmitted "more or less faithfully" from one generation to another. Thus, he adds, the "inheritance of mental health and mental ill health through the medium of family microculture is certainly no less important, and may well be far more important, than is their inheritance through the medium of genes."[45]

On the final page of his trilogy, Bowlby states his general position:

> Intimate attachments to other human beings are the hub around which a person's life revolves, not only when he is an infant or a toddler or a schoolchild but throughout his adolescence and his years of maturity as well, and on into old age. From these

intimate attachments a person draws his strength and enjoyment of life and, through what he contributes, he gives strength and enjoyment to others. These are matters about which current science and traditional wisdom are at one.[46]

John Bowlby—a Summary

John Bowlby's work must be taken as a whole and not perceived as merely a study of the responses of deprived children as observed in institutions. Nor should it be seen as merely the extrapolation from animal behavior of some processes which are then applied to the life of humans. Bowlby's work can be separated into two stages, but each informs the other. Bowlby would not have been drawn to Lorenz's work and the nature of imprinting in other species had he not studied separation in humans and the consequences of it. But the corollary is that his subsequent study of attachment helped him retrospectively to explain the significance of separations more fully.

1. Attachment behavior is any form of behavior that results in a person attaining or retaining proximity to some other differentiated and preferred individual. So long as the attachment figure remains accessible and responsive, the behavior may consist of little more than checking by eye or ear on the whereabouts of the figure and exchanging occasional glances and greetings. In certain circumstances, however, following or clinging to the attachment figure may occur and also calling or crying, which are likely to elicit her caregiving.

2. As a class of behavior with its own dynamic, attachment behavior can be seen to be distinct from feeding and sexual behavior and of at least equal importance in human life.

3. During the course of healthy development, attachment behavior leads to the development of affectional bonds or attachments, initially between child and parent and later between adult and adult.

There is a strong tendency for attachment behavior to become directed mainly towards one particular person, usually the child's natural mother, but this role can be taken effectively by others, providing a mother substitute behaves in a mothering way towards a child.

4. Mothering is a two-way process, characterized by love, responsiveness and continuity. Fathers usually play a supportive role to the central mother-child relationship. The family enables the mother-child relationship to flourish.

5. Whereas an attachment bond endures, the various forms of attachment behavior that contribute to it are active only when required. Attachments are formed more readily within a sensitive period that commences at about the end of three months; attachment behavior is still prominent in the third year.

6. The formation, maintenance, disruption and renewal of attachment relationships give rise to many of the most intense human emotions. Falling in love, loving someone and grieving the loss of a partner are all part of the process. Similarly, the threat of loss causes anxiety and actual loss gives rise to sorrow; both of these situations are likely to arouse anger. A strongly maintained bond is experienced as a source of security and the renewal of a bond as a source of joy. "Because such emotions are usually a reflection of the state of a person's affectional bonds, the psychology and psychopathology of emotion is found to be in large part the psychology and psychopathology of affectional bonds."[47]

7. Attachment behavior contributes to the individual's survival by keeping her in touch with her caretaker(s), thereby reducing the risk of her coming to harm; for example, from cold, hunger or drowning.

8. Behavior complementary to attachment behavior and serving a complementary function, that of protecting the attached individual, is care-giving (mothering). This is commonly shown by a parent, or other adult, towards a child or adolescent, but it is also shown by one adult towards another, especially in times of ill health, stress or old age.

9. Because attachment behavior is potentially active throughout life and has the vital biological function proposed, it is wrong to suppose that, when active in an adult, attachment behavior is indicative either of pathology or of regression to immature behavior.

10. Disturbed patterns of attachment behavior can be present at any age. One of the commonest forms of disturbance is the "over-ready elicitation of attachment behavior, resulting in anxious attachment."[48]

11. The principal determinants of the pathway along which an individual's attachment behavior develops, and of the pattern in which it becomes organized, are the experiences he has with his attachment figures during his years of immaturity—infancy, childhood and adolescence. Over these years, and indeed throughout life, the child—on the basis of her attachment experiences—develops internal working models of how the world of significant other persons meshes with the model of self.

12. The way in which an individual's attachment behavior becomes organized within her personality affects the pattern of affectional bonds she makes during her life. Because children tend unwittingly to identify with their parents, there is a tendency to behave in the same way towards their children when parents. A social cycle is therefore a distinct possibility.

Charles Rycroft, in a cogent summary of Bowlby's achievements, points to two simple consequences of Bowlby's work: "good mothering and a secure, happy home life form, therefore, the basis for an inner sense of security in later life," and the fact that "in our culture too many children experience too many separations from their mothers too young, at grave cost to their present and future happiness."[49] Bowlby's work has been presented here as the best model of what mothering is and should be, and as useful in explaining the problems of children (and society) around us. As we proceed we shall see that the model has its critics and its supporters. But when things do go wrong in the crucial formative years they are very difficult to put right.

3

How Right and Wrong Can You Be?

It appears that there is virtually no psychosocial adversity to which some children have not been subjected, yet later recovered, granted a radical change of circumstances.

Ann M. Clarke and A.D.B. Clarke, *Early Experience*

Prisons, mental hospitals, borstals and schools for the maladjusted, contain a high proportion of individuals who in childhood were unloved and rejected. Their number is high too among the chronically unemployable and among able misfits. Anger, hate, lack of concern for others and an inability to make mutually satisfactory relationships are common reactions to having been unloved and rejected.

Mia Kellmer Pringle, *The Needs of Children*

IN this chapter we look at some of the criticisms that have been leveled at the work of Bowlby and then consider some of the uses to which his work has been put by others. It must be said at the outset that the nature of "evidence" in this debate is suspect, as it is in any area of life, controversy and morality. We are using Bowlby's work here as an eminently sensible and plausible set of ideas to help produce an argument about the importance of mothering. We should begin by considering the nature of the "evidence" involved.

The "Truth" of Child Development Research

I make no apologies for being somewhat cynical about much of what passes for scholarly "evidence." In my opinion, much of such work is poor and somewhat misleading, but in one sense it is bound to be so, because of the subject matter—human life—and what I consider to be the inevitable problems of any inquiry into aspects of human life.

Humans are not inanimate objects and therefore cannot be studied "scientifically" in the way that minerals and chemicals may be. We act upon the world, we change our behavior over time, indeed we are often motivated unconsciously. The best we can hope for are plausible answers to our own subjective questions; if we claim anything else we will be in trouble. There is an unfortunate tendency in the human sciences to believe that all questions can be answered. "History shows that once people become psychologists of a particular school, they easily become imbued with an omnipotent sense of its ability to answer all questions," says David Ingleby.[1] Ingleby points to another particularly relevant weakness, which is partly to do with the obsession to measure or quantify: "It is obvious to almost everyone except developmental psychologists that childhood is an extremely emotional period—both for adults and children: yet social development is predominantly analysed in cognitive, not affective, terms."[2] Investigators, in the way they go about their research and in the manner in which they attempt to prove their hypotheses, invariably find what they are looking for—in other words they will ensure that their world view is not contaminated by contrary facts. A related tendency is the urge to falsify results, as Jack Tizard notes in his discussion of the late Sir Cyril Burt, of "intelligence-testing" fame. Sir Cyril Burt (1883–1971) was the first British educational psychologist (1912) and remained an influential figure to the end of his life. It now seems certain that in later life, from about 1950, he fabricated data on twin studies to support his views on intelligence. Burt's concern to fit reality into his conceptual framework meant that his interpretation of his "purported findings was also sometimes dubious"—to put it mildly.[3]

The point is an important one; researchers in the contentious area of child development invariably find what they are looking for because of the moral choices they have already made about what is important and what is "right." An appropriate example of this is Margaret Mead's *Coming of Age in Samoa,* in which she claimed both that a relaxed attitude towards adolescent sex existed on the island and that the whole Samoan system of child-rearing made such an attitude possible.

Margaret Mead herself described vividly the picture she "saw":

> In matters of sex the ten-year-olds are equally sophisticated, although they witness sex activities only surreptitiously, since all expressions of affection are rigorously barred in public. . . . The only sort of demonstration which ever occurs in public is of the horseplay variety between young people whose affections are not really involved. This romping is particularly prevalent in groups of women, often taking the form of playfully snatching at the sex organs.
>
> But the lack of privacy within the houses, where mosquito netting marks off purely formal walls about the married couples, and the custom of young lovers of using the palm groves for their rendezvous, makes it inevitable that children should see intercourse, often and between many different people . . . scouring the village palm groves in search of lovers is one of the recognized forms of amusement for the ten-year-olds.
>
> Samoan children have complete knowledge of the human body and its functions, owing to the custom of little children going unclothed, the scant clothing of adults, the habit of bathing in the sea, the use of the beach as a latrine, and the lack

of privacy in sexual life. They also have a vivid understanding of the nature of sex. Masturbation is an all but universal habit, beginning at the age of six or seven. . . . Theoretically it is discontinued with the beginning of heterosexual activity and resumed again only in periods of enforced continence. Among grown boys and girls casual homosexual practice also supplants it to a certain extent. Boys masturbate in groups, but among little girls it is a more individualistic, secretive practice.[4]

Samoan children, Mead claims, never learn "the meaning of a strong attachment to one person," and because early childhood does not provide them with "violent feelings," there are no such feelings to be rediscovered through adolescence. The Samoan family, she claims, is "just a long series of people of different ages, all somehow related to one another." This means that Samoan children are "given no sense of belonging to a small intimate biological family," and so "do not form strong affectional ties with their parents." Instead, "filial affection is diffused among a large group of relatives," with the result that "in Samoa the child owes no emotional allegiance to its father and mother," and children "do not think of an own mother who always protects them," but rather of "a group of adults all of whom have their interests somewhat but not too importantly at heart."

Sex without guilt and a bevy of adults to help with growing up. But was this idyll a true account of life in Samoa? This is the question that Derek Freeman set out to answer, and in *Margaret Mead and Samoa* he states that Mead's entire account of adolescence in Samoa is markedly at "variance with the facts of Samoan existence." Freeman found not a relaxed sexual adolescence, but rather much rape, violence and incest.

In terms of the relationships Samoan children had with their parents, Freeman reports that

attachment behavior in Samoan infants has all of the characteristics described by Bowlby. In Samoa, as in other human populations, an infant during its first year of life becomes behaviorally attached to its caretaker, whoever she or he may be.[5]

Freeman conducted a simple experiment designed to test Mead's claim that in Samoa "filial affection is diffused among a large group of relatives," by having the women of an extended family walk away from an infant one at a time. There was an "agitated reaction" when the infant was separated from its own mother (and her alone) and this, according to Freeman, demonstrated that "attachment in Samoa, as elsewhere, is with but rare exceptions monotropic." Again, when one particular mother moved away from all the younger children of an extended family, it was only her own children who showed distress. Freeman concludes that "the primary bond between mother and child is very much a part of the biology of Samoans, as it is of all humans."[6]

Both Mead and Freeman were in Samoa; both observed and interviewed Samoans; both were interested in Samoan child-rearing; but they came to radically different conclusions. This is not a mystery; it is a case of normal science—they chose their informants, they framed their questions, they observed particular patterns of behavior, all of which was designed to prove what they had set out to prove.

Criticizing Bowlby

Bowlby has always been singled out for criticism—often of things he has not said, or did not mean—yet other theorists of the same period were saying much the same thing. Donald Winnicott, for example, possibly the most famous English psychoanalyst, talked in a 1957 radio broadcast of the "ordinary good mother with her husband in support," and what an immense contribution she makes "to society" simply through being "devoted to her infant." Interestingly enough, Winnicott asks:

> Is not this contribution of the devoted mother un-recognized precisely because it is immense? If this contribution is accepted it follows that every man or woman who is sane, every man or woman who has the feeling of being a person in the world, and for whom the world means something, every happy person, is in infinite debt to a woman.[7]

Elsewhere, Winnicott tells us that healthy, independent and society-minded individuals depend, as "human babies," on the good start "assured in nature by the existence of the bond between the baby's mother and the baby, the thing called love." As if to create guilt, Winnicott adds: "If you love your baby he or she is getting a good start."[8]

Erik Erikson's classic *Childhood and Society,* originally published in 1950, made much the same sort of observation and assertion as Bowlby. On the subject of the importance of trust, for example, he argues that the "infant's first social achievement" is her willingness to let the mother out of sight "without undue anxiety or rage, because she has become an inner certainty as well as an outer predictability." Erikson adds that the firm establishment of enduring patterns for the solution of the fundamental conflict of "basic trust versus basic mistrust in mere existence" is the first task of "maternal care." He goes on to say that "the amount of trust derived from earliest infantile experience does not seem to depend on absolute qualities of food or demonstrations of love, but rather on the quality of the maternal relationship."[9]

If Bowlby was not alone in his approach to mothering and the parent-child relationship, why did his work in particular attract so much attention? One simple explanation is that much of his writing is clear and accessible—especially his earlier work—and therefore reached a much wider public than most psychological and psychoanalytic work. More importantly, his work had direct implications for practical issues, such as preschool care—even if Bowlby did not make them himself. He borrowed ideas from the (still) controversial area of the study of animal behavior. He appeared to be telling women and mothers what to do. His conclusions about the consequences of painful early experiences may have appeared unpalatable. And finally, there is in Bowlby's work, as with all psychoanalytically inspired writing, a tone of pessimism.

Human Animals

Other theorists have no problems in comparing humans with other animals. The anthropologist Robin Fox considers that humans have an immense capacity for illusion, that in fact cultures are "massive con jobs, and the variations are as unlimited as the imagination of man itself." Fox himself has no illusions about the manner in which we can compare human animals with other species (italics added):

> *The accumulation of facts on this issue is overwhelming.* It is a basic ground rule for any primate species that, if the object is healthy and effective adults, the mother and child have to be associated safely and securely through the critical period of birth and at least to the point where the children become independently mobile.[10]

Bowlby himself has never been so definite in his views; he has borrowed ideas from the study of other species in order to produce a model of how he considers attachments develop and function in the human species. He has always seen his model as one which will inevitably be modified in the normal way.

Bowlby certainly is not as crude in his comparative analysis as his mentor Darwin. In the latter's "Biographical Sketch of an Infant," based on his own children and published in 1877, he observed that when eleven months old, his son would push away and beat a plaything if he did not want it: "I presume that the beating was an instinctive sign of anger, like the snapping of the jaws by a young crocodile just out of the egg, and not that he imagined he could hurt the plaything."

Judy Bernal and Martin Richards complain that Bowlby's approach, which sets the relationship between mother and infant "so firmly in the context of the Primate heritage, necessarily underplays the specifically human characteristics of the relationship."[11] What precisely do they mean? Bowlby certainly borrowed ideas from the behavior of other species to see how they *might* apply to humans. What can be more human than the characteristics he describes as being essential to the development of a two-way mother–infant relationship—love and responsiveness, for example. Blurton Jones argues that if frequent feeding is a means of developing some kind of social relationship, particularly an early tie between mother and child, there would be support from comparative studies for Bowlby's suggestion that suckling contributes in some way to the child's attachment to its mother.

> The comparative evidence makes it highly probable, although the evidence is very incomplete, that Bowlby is right in saying that suckling is in some ways an adaptation for developing a close mother–infant attachment. The association in the mammals between frequent feeding and a following or carrying system of child care is not nutritionally necessary, but rapid onset of hunger and satiation in the baby would be a simple mechanism for ensuring that it stays with the mother.[12]

Richards chides Bowlby on his timing of the sensitive period for attachment: "separation was not thought to be important for very young infants" because newborns were often assumed to be too immature to be much influenced by their environment, provided, of course, that they received the basic requirements such as food and warmth. But, Richards adds, with the growing appreciation of the capabilities of newborns this has seemed less and less reasonable. Richards concentrates on the impact of hospital births and the inevitable separations in the days that follow. Adverse effects have been noted in the early development of infants following such separations as periods of incubation, and Richards suggests that it is what such experiences do to the *mother* that is important: the factor of self-confidence—the more contact the mother has, and perhaps even more importantly, the more responsibility she is allowed for the care of the child, the sooner the mother becomes self-confident and assured about her ability to look after the baby; separation could influence a mother by giving her an implicit model of how she should care for her baby—"if she does not see her baby for a day or so after delivery and then only at a brief feed each four hours (as is not unusual in American hospitals) the mother may then leave the hospital with the idea that this is the natural and expected pattern of the relationship which she should continue when she gets home." For Richards, if such factors change the mother's relationship with her baby, they are just as likely to influence the baby's development also. [13]

Such "findings" are valuable. They in no sense affect the validity of Bowlby's model, however. To begin with, Bowlby would not deny that experiences earlier than the "sensitive period," in which attachment processes operate more readily, can have an effect. Nor would he consider it unimportant that certain practices hinder a mother's relationship with her infant. Bowlby has always stressed the importance of a continuous relationship. However, it is specifically attachments—which for good reasons take time to develop—that are both the source and cause of either emotional security or insecurity and all that follows.

Mother Is Not Unique

The other, more important, criticisms of Bowlby's work are summarized by Barbara Tizard as follows.[14]

1. Separation does not in itself cause harmful effects.
2. The mother-child relationship is not of unique importance in development.
3. Day care is not in itself damaging.
4. The child's own characteristics affect the mother's behavior.
5. The early years are not decisive for development.

Later chapters will examine some of these criticisms in greater detail, but here I would like to comment on them more generally. Perhaps the most widespread criticism is that the early years are not decisive for development: the possibly deleterious effects of early experience, in other words, are reversible.

The first point is, quite simply, that Bowlby never claimed that adverse early experiences are *irreversible*. For Bowlby, adverse early experiences—especially of a gross nature—leave an imprint on personality and affect the ability to form or otherwise to sustain relationships. That is plausible enough. Psychologists and philosophers of every persuasion believe in the importance of the formative years. Freud for example believed that "neuroses are only acquired during early childhood (up to the age of six), even though their symptoms may not make their appearance until much later . . . analytic experience has convinced us of the complete truth of the common assertion that the child is psychologically father of the man and that the events of his first years are of paramount importance for his whole subsequent life." Plato, much earlier, asserted that the "first step, as you know, is always what matters most, particularly when we are dealing with those who are young and tender. That is the time when they are taking shape and when any impression we choose to make leaves a permanent mark."

An extreme position on the matter is found in the work of Ann Clarke and A. Clarke, who claim, in the belief that they are criticizing Bowlby, that *"it appears that there is virtually no psychosocial adversity to which some children have not been subject, yet later recovered, granted a radical change of circumstances."*[15] Children can, of course, "recover" from all sorts of deprivations and adversity in the same way that children are adaptable. But do children have any choice in these matters? Clarke and Clarke miss both the content and more importantly the spirit of Bowlby's arguments. Bowlby, too, believes that children can continue to function following a traumatic separation, and can recover, but he would argue that such an experience nonetheless has an impact. And it can become cumulative. The child may indeed function adequately, but happiness is that much more difficult to achieve. And the child is more vulnerable to later stresses. More importantly, the spirit of Bowlby's work is all about prevention through an understanding of causes. This is the crucial and significant knowledge we require. It seems indisputable that the early years, and the experiences we have as children, especially in relation to our parents, are the formative years. No one, including Bowlby, is saying that later events in life cannot have an effect: of course they can. But what happens to us in later life—divorce and anxiety states, to take but two examples—is in no way unrelated to what happens to us in these early years—not only in terms of causation, but in terms of our vulnerability to certain events, and the form and severity of such events.

An interesting example of both the degree of "reversibility" possible and the extent to which "the mother-child relationship is not of unique importance in development" is that of a study of child survivors of the holocaust.

Anna Freud and Sophie Dann "studied" six young German-Jewish orphans, whose parents were deported to Poland and killed in the gas chambers soon after their children's birth. Freud and Dann graphically describe the next few years of the children's lives:

During the first year of life, the children's experiences differed; they were handed on from one refuge to another, until they arrived individually, at ages varying from approximately six to twelve months, in the concentration camp of Tereszin. There they became inmates of the Ward of Motherless Children, were conscientiously cared for and medically supervised, within the limits of the current restrictions of food and living space. They had no toys and their only facility for outdoor life was a bare yard. The Ward was staffed by nurses and helpers, themselves inmates of the concentration camp and as such, undernourished and over-worked. Since Tereszin was a transit camp, deportations were frequent. Approximately two to three years after arrival, in the spring of 1945, when liberated by the Russians, the six children, with others, were taken to a Czech castle where they were given special care and were lavishly fed. After one month's stay, the six were included in a transport of 300 older children and adolescents, all of them survivors from concentration camps, the first of 1000 children for whom the British Home Office had granted permits of entry. They were flown to England in bombers and arrived in August 1945 in a carefully set-up reception camp in Windermere, Westmoreland, where they remained for two months. When this reception camp was cleared and the older children distributed to various hostels and training places, it was thought wise to leave the six youngsters together, to remove them from the commotion which is inseparable from the life of a large children's community and to provide them with peaceful, quiet surroundings where, for a year at least, they could adapt themselves gradually to a new country, a new language, and the altered circumstances of their lives.[16]

These six children were, without doubt, "rejected" infants in that they were deprived of mother love, stability in their relationships and their surroundings. They were passed from one hand to another during the first year, lived in an age group instead of a family during their second and third years, and were uprooted again three times during their fourth year. Their parents had been killed and they were raised in what could have only been an atmosphere of catastrophe. In those extremely abnormal circumstances, the children developed unusually strong ties with each other, which seem to have had a protective influence. Not surprisingly, the children suffered emotional problems—they were hypersensitive, restless, aggressive, difficult to handle. But, as Freud and Dann observe, they were "neither deficient, delinquent nor psychotic." Or, as Michael Rutter puts it, while the children showed various emotional problems, they did not show the "gross disturbances which might be expected as a result of the total loss of mothering experiences and gross rejection that they had suffered."[17] And Sarah Moskovitz's follow-up study, in which she interviewed some of the survivors, concluded that—despite certain emotional and personality problems— "those child survivors who are now in their mid-forties to mid-fifties have much to contribute, particularly to the study of resilience"; many made "adaptions that are not only impressive but inspiring."[18]

The Freud and Dann study is often used against Bowlby, arguing that further attachments can develop and moreover that they can be crucially important to development. Bowlby, however, has always maintained that although a child invariably has more than one attachment, there is nevertheless a preferential figure, a principal attachment figure. Any attachment, according to Bowlby, is better than none. Rudolph Schaffer and Peggy Emerson have in effect argued for a *hierarchy* of attachment figures. While an infant may show some form of attachment towards a number of different individuals at any one time, these attachments are unlikely to be of the same intensity. There is usually some sort of hierarchy, in which the individual at the top, to whom the most intense attachment is shown, may be described as the infant's principal object. This is completely compatible with Bowlby's position.

Bowlby has argued that it is both likely and preferable that the infant's principal attachment figure should be the natural mother, but that this role *can* be taken effectively by others. Although somewhat more optimistic than Bowlby, Tom Bower probably summarizes the issue of "reversibility" well when he asserts that

> good maternal care in infancy, care which allows the develop-
> ment of deep and intimate communicational routines, seems to
> produce *irreversible* good effects on the developing child. The
> lack of this kind of care produces bad effects, but effects which
> are *reversible* however difficult the process may be.[19]

On whether separation in itself causes harmful effects, there is great controversy. Research into the question is neces-sarily an unfinished business. Michael Rutter, in his detailed summary of the evidence in *Maternal Deprivation Reassessed*, points to

> the continuing accumulation of evidence showing the impor-
> tance of deprivation and disadvantage as influences on children's
> psychological development. Bowlby's (1951) original argu-
> ments on that score have been amply confirmed. However . . . it
> is now very clear that deprivation involves a most hetero-
> geneous group of adversities which operate through several
> quite different psychological mechanisms. Thus, insofar as
> deprivation is a causal factor, the acute distress syndrome some-
> times shown during admission to hospital or to a residential
> nursery is probably due in part to an interference with attach-
> ment behaviour and in part to the effects of a strange and
> frightening environment, with the disturbances after return
> home probably due in part to the adverse effects of separation
> on parent–child relationships . . . conduct disorders are in part a

response to family discord and disturbed interpersonal relationships; and affectionless psychopathy may be a consequence of
abnormal early bonding. New research has confirmed that,
although an important stress, separation is not *the* crucial factor
in most varieties of deprivation.[20]

Bowlby, in his desire to present his model as an all-encompass-
ing one, did fail to fill in some of the detail—and indeed got
some things quite wrong. For example, he discussed in considerable detail the politics of the family—who did what to
whom and why and when—but he did not specify whether
boys and girls differed significantly in terms of various
responses to their mothers or principal attachment figures.

Nursery Wars

"The Bowlby 'doctrine' served to legitimize the re-establish-
ment of traditional social patterns, which had become rather
more flexible between 1939–45 as a result of women's employment in the war effort, whereby mothers primarily provided
care for their children," writes Helen Graham, who adds that
"many war time nurseries were closed down and the establishment of creches was discouraged, making it difficult for many
mothers to continue working."[21]

This is another accusation commonly made against Bowlby,
namely that popular psychology assisted a postwar government in its decision-making activities in the areas of child care.
Denise Riley, in *War in the Nursery*, although not a Bowlby
supporter, suggests, quite rightly, that such a view is somewhat naïve: if only life was that dramatic, and indeed if only
"ideas" had that potency:

Certainly, the general spirit of Bowlbyism in Britain in the
mid-1950s would have made the question of the provision of

child care for working mothers almost unaskable—but this is a quite different proposition from putting the events of 1945 down to psychology and psychoanalysis. Yet if the psychology of the sanctity of the mother and child in the home did not occasion the closing of war nurseries, what did? To say that psychology and government were not in an unholy alliance to return women to the home is not to exonerate either, but to launch into a more mundane story—of misrepresentations, imaginative failures, evasions and indifference: less highly coloured, but no less deadly in its effects.[22]

Naima Browne argues that many women did indeed return to their homes. Nonetheless, although some did so because they felt that the jobs should be "for the men," and some were undoubtedly compelled to do so by inadequate child care facilities, many women probably gave up work after having made rational decisions based on their knowledge of the realities of female employment—e.g., low wages, lengthy journeys, tedious jobs and long shifts. She adds that another influencing factor was whether or not any particular area had a tradition of female employment.

The policy-makers' attitudes, however, were heavily influenced by the expectation that women and children were naturally going to be at home. There was also, moreover, an element of hypocrisy on the part of government. As Browne comments, rather than wanting all women to return to their homes, the government was in the position of "desperately requiring women's labour in certain industries that would help Britain's sluggish economy."[23] Nursery provision was seen as a means of luring women to work—parliamentary debates reveal that many individuals were not convinced of the value of nursery education—yet when the needs of young children were balanced against the needs of the economy, the economy won: "In normal times, the proper place for young children is in the home, and however good a day nursery may be, it cannot equal a good home environment. But times are not normal . . . it is quite useless the government appealing to mothers to go to work unless they make provision for looking after the children."[24] Day nurseries were, to the MP quoted here, obviously second best. Nonetheless, in order to end clothes rationing and improve textile exports, he was prepared to let the nation's under-fives receive second-best care. However, as I will argue later, political solutions are inadequate to the problems we really face.

It is time now to turn to the usefulness of attachment theory—apart from its obvious application in explaining the consequences of early experiences.

The Importance of Attachments

In Bowlby's own work, attachments are the "hub of life," from which a person gains strength to enjoy and take part in life. Nothing less will do.

It is clear from Bowlby's writing that secure attachments enable the infant to explore away from the mother knowing that there is a secure base to which to return. As Carl Corter puts it, apart from the mother's importance in the "attachment relationship," she also plays a crucial role in "her facilitation of the infant's exploration of his world outside the infant-mother interplay."[25] Clearly this is also important in more nonemotional areas such as learning. No one can learn if they are constantly in a state of insecurity: it is impossible to concentrate. However, the relationship of emotion to reason, or emotion to mind, is one with which academic psychologists have had extreme difficulty in dealing. They have not known where one begins and the other finishes, and moreover have been unable to measure sufficiently the qualities expressed in the term "emotion." I have no intention of resolving the difficulty here. On the contrary, I think that the dichotomy between reason and emotion is a false one. As Pascal said, the "heart has its reasons, which are quite unknown to the head."

Jerome Bruner, in an essay on poverty and childhood, makes the obvious connection with learning (italics added):

> Human young more than any other perhaps, are dependent on a consistent caretaker who is there with warmth, certainty and effectiveness. *It is in interaction with a caretaker that much of earliest learning occurs.* A well-informed, decently satisfied and hopeful caretaker is worth a pound of cure.[26]

Children who learn to read at home, before they begin formal education, are an obvious example. F. Smith, on the other hand, in *Attachment of the Young* focuses on the importance of attachments for feelings of self-esteem, feelings of course which have their origins in the development of internal working models of the world of significant others and self, and argues that it is this sense of self-esteem which is so important.

> The sense of attachment so necessary in early life becomes, with greater awareness of the social environment, a sense of solicitude, the conviction that someone cares about oneself. If the conviction is achieved, an important source of reassurance and orientation is available to help in meeting the feelings of doubt, anxiety and guilt, associated with growing up, until the maturing personality has acquired the width of orientation to ensure a measure of independence. If this conviction is not achieved, despite opportunities which may occur apart from parents, the probability of a satisfactory adjustment to society is lowered.[27]

An area which has been extensively researched by attachment theorists is that of depression and its relationship to the separation and loss of attachments. George Brown and Tirril Harris's *Social Origins of Depression,* a study of depression in working-class women in London, is one example of research that stimulated further work on the subject. They discovered that the experience of loss can contribute causally to depressive disorders in any one of three ways. First, as a *provoking* agent which increases the risk of disorder developing and determines the time at which it does so; a majority of women in the study had suffered a major loss from death or for other reasons, such as the loss of spouse through divorce, during the nine months prior to the onset of illness. Secondly, loss can contribute as a *vulnerability* factor which increases an individual's sensitivity to such events; in Brown and Harris's study, loss of the mother before the age of eleven is of particular significance. Thirdly, loss can contribute as a factor that influences both the *severity* and the *form* of any depressive disorder that may develop.

Loss and related types of event, however, were not the only forms of personal experience found by Brown and Harris to be contributing causally to depressive disorders. Like losses, these other factors could be divided into those that trigger depression and those that make an individual more vulnerable—more sensitive—to the effects of separation and loss. Among the former were certain sorts of family events that, although lying outside their definition of a severe event, were nonetheless very worrying or distressing and which had persisted for two or more years. Among the factors that seemed to have increased a woman's vulnerability were the absence in her life of any intimate personal relationships, the presence of three or more children under fourteen to be cared for, and no outside employment.

The prevalence of depression in mothers with young children has clear implications for the study of attachments and attachment behavior. Andrea Pound notes that the emphasis in most attachment research to date has been on the "effects of the physical separation of the child from the mother in the early years,"[28] although Bowlby himself has always emphasized the importance of the quality as well as the continuity in time of the mother-child relationship: "What is believed to be essential for mental health is that the infant and young child should experience a warm, intimate, and continuous relationship with his mother (or permanent mother-substitute) in which both find satisfaction and enjoyment."[29] The mother's responsiveness and sensitivity to the baby's signals have been shown to be associated with the security of attachment.

Pound claims that threats of abandonment or of suicide may be even more damaging to the child's sense of secure attachment than physical separation; they may compound the effects of actual separation when it occurs. High degrees of anxiety and "overdependence" have also been found in children who have been subject to parents' irritability or disparaging remarks. Unresponsiveness, irritability and suicidal threats are all commonly found in depressed patients. These are behaviors to which we can assume the young child of a depressed mother is frequently exposed, and which result in insecure attachment. Pound concludes her own research as follows:

> Depression in the mothers of young children has been shown to be a common disturbance and one that is highly associated with psychiatric disorder in children. The effects on them are likely to be severe, but will vary according to the type of depression, the child's temperament, and the alternative sources of nurture in the family environment. . . . The implications for preventive psychiatry of such a widespread hazard to healthy child development cannot be underestimated. They are comparable to those of early loss or separation to which attachment theorists have long paid deserved attention.[30]

I have tried to stress that Bowlby's notion of a cycle of deprivation is a social cycle—patterns of interaction the child has unwittingly identified which are transmitted from one generation to another. Too many critics believe that Bowlby, and others who argue in a similar fashion, are really talking about a genetic cycle. A small number of families *do* become trapped in cycles of deprivation and often their own behavior contributes to the continuation of this. However, such transmitted behavior is very much socially produced, because at each stage of each generation no one has bothered to intervene and demonstrate a different way of living. Moreover, such families invariably suffer multiple deprivations. Even if their own behavior is not the direct cause, such families will suffer deprivations of resources, material well-being and power.

The cycles of deprivation most frequently referred to are those that lead to the abuse of children. This is an extremely contentious issue, and from the outset we must state the obvious: that the majority of parents at one time or another have felt like abusing their children, whether physically or psychologically. As Bowlby continually points out, the most important occupation in the world ("mothering") is the most difficult one. However, those individuals who take one step further and actually abuse their children in physical, sexual and hence psychological ways—especially in extreme cases—demand a further explanation. Amidst the understandable horror we should feel on experiencing or reading of such cases, and the endless moralizing we hear on the subject, Schaffer's comments seem plausible:

> Some facts about such cases are now, however, beginning to emerge. In particular, it is widely agreed that violence usually results from the combination of three forces in the parents' lives: emotional immaturity which makes it difficult for them to deal with stress; various financial, social and occupational problems which they find insoluble; and finally some characteristic of the battered child that singles him out as a likely victim.[31]

All three factors can be culled from Bowlby's work, and it must be reiterated that Bowlby himself has always urged social and economic assistance to those suffering from inequality. Vincent Fontana, in *Somewhere a Child Is Crying,* an account of the hundreds of thousands of American children who are killed or injured by their parents annually, describes the social cyclical nature of abuse quite graphically yet realistically, arguing that patterns of physical and sexual abuse are all too easily transmitted from one generation to the next, unless something intervenes to break the vicious circle.

> The sexually abused little girl grows up to marry or cohabit with a man who sexually abuses their children; the incestuous father begets an incestuous or promiscuous son or daughter; the adult sexual-psychopath frequently turns out to have been the product of an undesirable sexual union or the victim of childhood seduction. [32]

For many, these arguments, like Bowlby's, appear to "blame the victim" too much, or more specifically to take the socioeconomic factors involved insufficiently into account. In my view, however, nothing could be further from the truth. It is certainly important to create just societies; societies in which people feel that they have an impact on the world, that what they do matters, that they are not deprived of resources and therefore that they do not suffer material deprivation, that they do not suffer from prejudice of race or gender, that they live in a society that cares for others—"from each according to his abilities, to each according to his needs." But there are no political points to be scored in denying the existence of families who are trapped in cycles of abuse, or in denying the continual potential of such families to exist. We can desire both the "just and good society," and want to recognize, intervene and eliminate such families engaged in such cycles, without doing either view a disservice. Both desires are indissolubly linked.

Addendum

Freud and Darwin are the inspiration behind Bowlby's work. As Bowlby's work progressed, the ideas of ethology became more prominent. But Freud, with his emphasis on the primacy of the formative years and the mental dynamics of the personality, has continued to influence Bowlby. Bowlby's work has taken him away from basic psychoanalytic ideas through his liaison with ethology, but also—and fundamentally—because of his reluctance to discuss or use the concept of the unconscious. As he himself recently put it, "I don't believe in 'the' unconscious, no. I believe that very many mental processes are unconscious." In a 1986 interview he elaborated on this point:

> Most of what goes on in the internal world is a more or less accurate reflection of what an individual has experienced recently or long ago in the external world . . . if a child sees his mother as a very loving person, the chances are that his mother is a very loving person. If he sees her as a very rejecting person, the chances are she is a very rejecting person . . . [and] a child has a very confused picture, but it's a replica of what is experienced.[33]

One of the reasons which explains why Bowlby found Darwin and ethology more illuminating than Freud on the process of attachment, separation and loss is Freud's own quite unusual position towards such processes.

When Freud lost his own father in 1896 he commented: "I feel now as if I had been torn up by the roots." But father loss was not all that Freud suffered in way of separation and loss. He lost his brother Julius when he himself was eighteen months old, he suffered from the abrupt dismissal of his nanny for theft when he was two and a half years old, and he also suffered from being separated from his mother on a number of occasions in childhood—when she was ill with tuberculosis. Although, as David Aberbach observes, Freud's discovery of the effects of loss on his dreams was a crucial factor in the development of psychoanalysis, he nonetheless made "little immediate use of this discovery in evolving a theory of loss and separation." Aberbach, in a brilliant essay on "loss and dreams," also describes the effect of childhood separation, and other family matters, on the life of Jung, also as seen through the medium of his dreams.[34] On the night before his mother's death, Jung dreamt that a wild huntsman had commanded a gigantic wolfhound to carry away a human soul. The dream aroused intense fear because, Jung explains, the Wild Huntsman was Wotan, or the devil: Jung had dreamt, in effect, that his mother (the "human soul") had been carried off to hell by the devil.

As Aberbach argues, the anticipation of his mother's death (she was by this time old and ill) seems to have revived in full force Jung's childhood ambivalence towards her. In his early years she had suffered from mental illness and been treated in hospital in Basel. The nature of her illness and the separation had a profound, long-lasting effect on Jung. "I was deeply troubled by my mother's being away. From then on, I always felt mistrustful when the word 'love' was spoken. The feeling I associated with 'woman' was for a long time that of innate unreliability." As he grew older, Jung in fact conceived of his mother as having two personalities, one loving and reliable, the other unpredictable and frightening: "There was an enormous difference between my mother's two personalities. That was why as a child I often had anxiety dreams. By the day she was a loving mother, but at night she seemed uncanny."

As Aberbach notes, Jung's "dual attitude to his mother, formed by her duality," was sharpened by his parents' incompatibility: "My parents' marriage was not a happy one, but full of trials and difficulties and tests of patience." His parents were sleeping apart and Jung was sharing a room with his father when he had a grisly hallucination:

> From the door to my mother's room came frightening influences. At night Mother was strange and mysterious. One night I saw coming from her door a faintly luminous, indefinite figure whose head detached itself from the neck and floated along in front of it, in the air, like a little moon. Immediately

another head was produced and again detached itself. The process was repeated six or seven times.[35]

Aberbach suggests that the apparition of the beheaded figure, coming, as it does, from the mother's bedroom, could betray violent impulses and death wishes towards the mother. But the actual death of this Medusa-like mother provoked in Jung conflicting emotions, in response to her own duality and its lifelong effect on him. On receiving the news of her death, Jung went home.

> I had a feeling of great grief, but in my heart of hearts I could not be mournful, and this for a strange reason: during the entire journey I continually heard dance music, laughter, and jollity, as though a wedding were being celebrated. . . . One side of me had a feeling of warmth and joy, and the other of terror and grief.

Jung's reaction of joy, as well as grief, to his mother's death could be ascribed to the fulfillment of his unconscious desire that she should die and go to hell. Aberbach adds that Jung's dream and his interpretation of it provide insight not only into the nature of his bond with his mother, but also into some of the personal motivations underlying his psychological system.[36]

Could the loss of, or separation from, a father possibly cause as much of a reaction? Indeed, are fathers important?

4

Will Daddy (or Day Care) Do?

Essentially, because men do not raise children, all mothers are raising children "alone." But a single mother leads a different life from a married one, and a family with no grown men in the house is more different yet. The position of divorced, widowed, or never-married mothers is made more difficult than that of women who remain married by the socioeconomic structures of patriarchy and the continuing presence and influence of the idealized nuclear family—that still-lively notion that we all live on the set of "Father Knows Best."

Judith Arcana, *Every Mother's Son*

AS Bowlby himself has pointed out on a number of occasions, he has devoted little of his time to the study of men and fathers. For Bowlby at least, there were good reasons for this—predominantly the fact that the "normal" home of the 1940s and 1950s was more in keeping with the (still) mythical image of the nuclear family. There were dramatically fewer divorces, fewer "single-parent families" headed by women and hence fewer cases of "father loss." Above all, there were fewer working mothers: the division of labor in the household was firmly established—mother at home, father at work. Studies of children's relationships were invariably studies of mother-child relationships as long as the mother was the prime caretaker. Bowlby followed suit. The situation is now quite different. In the United States there are currently over five and a half million girls under eighteen years of age growing up without fathers around, for one reason or another.

Elyce Wakerman's *Father Loss* is a study of such "girls" who have lost their fathers either through desertion, death, divorce or indeed those who have never ever known their fathers. Her approach to the subject is essentially psychological; social and economic factors play very little part in her analysis. Nonetheless, *Father Loss* is a compelling account of the inevitable psychological damage such losses are likely to cause. On the death of a father, for example, Wakerman argues that a daughter is "suddenly deprived of the first man she ever loved." She carries that rejection with her for the remainder of her life, and an early "acceptance of her loss is invaluable, just as resonances in her adulthood are inevitable."[1] Wakerman compares the "sorrow" felt for the dead father with the "pain" of the girl left without a father through divorce, and argues that whether "fostered by the absolute finality of death or the false hope following divorce, the womanhood of fatherless daughters was given shape by the loss of love." Wakerman's conclusion argues for the importance of fathers.

> Compared to 14 per cent of women from intact homes, one third of the married fatherless women in our study have been married more than once. Whether father was indifferent or superhuman in his ability to love, he left a void that we feel compelled to fill. Lacking both the experience and observation of a successful male–female relationship, we grapple with our misconceptions until, finally, many of us do get it right.[2]

All of this, however, is based on the experiences of women who have not suffered economically to any great degree and who have invariably (in the cases of loss through death and divorce) had positive and rewarding relationships with their fathers. Is that the common experience for most women? What do we know about fathers?

The "First Intruder" into the "Magic Circle"

In recent years fathers have entered the limelight a little more. They feature, for example, centrally in many popular accounts of family life, in films like *Kramer vs. Kramer, Paris, Texas* and *Table for Five* (and somewhat more insidiously in *E. T.*), in articles and books. As psychologist Charlie Lewis points out, "Widespread comment was made about John Lennon's parenting role shortly before his death, and now Prince Charles's involvement receives frequent coverage."[3]

Historically, of course, fathers were not assigned a central role in child care in the pages of advice manuals, let alone within academic developmental psychology. As Hardyment puts it: "Lacking breasts and being out to work all day were potent disadvantages. . . . Psychoanalysts approved of an increased fatherly presence, pointing out that his absence too often left little boys without a point for imitation."[4] Hardyment observes that in the United States the matter of a greater fatherly role in the family was encouraged by the "fear of matriarchy" which emerged openly after the Second World War. Edward A. Strecher, for example, was inspired in 1946 to write *Their Mothers' Sons* by the "cold, hard facts that 1,825,000 men were rejected from military service because of psychiatric disorders, that almost another 600,000 were discharged from the army for neuro-psychiatric reasons or their equivalent, and that fully 500,000 more attempted to evade the draft." These men were regarded as immature, whereas maturity, Strecher asserted, was the result of early background, environment, training and unselfish parental love. For Strecher, the problem was the presence of "overpossessive and dominant mothers" who failed to loosen the "psychological apronstrings that bound their children to them." Phyllis Hostler's *The Child's World* also discussed "shared parenting," and although she described the father as "the first intruder" into the "magic circle" of mother and child, Hostler nonetheless allowed him the privilege of fetching diapers, supplying extra pocket money and supervising the Sunday walk.

Certainly the father is mentioned more in contemporary advice manuals and in discussions of developmental psychology, but the question we have to consider is, *how much more involved* is the modern father in child care?

The "New Man"—a Journalist's Fiction

John and Elizabeth Newson, in their classic *Patterns of Infant Care,* a study of Nottingham, and optimistic postwar Britain, paint a particularly sympathetic portrait of the modern father.

> The cinema owners and the brewers may well lament over the declining clientele: parents of young families are neglecting the evening-out habits of their courting days; both mother and father are becoming home-centred, finding their interests, their occupation and their entertainment within the family circle. At a time when he has more money in his pocket, and more leisure on which to spend it, than ever before, the head of the household chooses to sit at his own fireside, a baby on his knee and a feeding bottle in his hand: the modern father's place is in the home.[5]

Does the postmodern father believe that his place is in the home, with baby on lap and feeding bottle in hand?

In *Becoming a Father,* Charlie Lewis suggests that, unlike Bowlby, a number of psychologists—including himself— believe the study of fathers to be most important in understanding the modern family. Lewis undertook extensive research into fatherhood to test the hypothesis that contemporary men are increasingly involved in family life.

Lewis argues, in a vein not dissimilar to Bowlby, that the emotional involvement of fathers appears to change over the first year of the child's life. The "ambiguous nature of fatherhood" is accentuated. The father is simultaneously engrossed with the newborn child but also feels excluded from the mother-infant bond—an echo of Hostler's "magic circle"—since the father's practical role in child care seems to him to be limited. As the year goes by and the child develops more social skills, fathers become more involved. This "playmate" role, according to Lewis, comes "naturally to fathers," and arises appropriately enough at a time when men are at home and the child needs, and demands, attention.[6]

It is difficult to know what exactly Lewis is claiming when he says that the "playmate" role comes naturally to fathers. It is probably more likely that this role is the one chosen by men in their decisions about what to do in child care. It is a role which is comfortable to men. But as Ann Oakley suggests, this role is in itself not necessarily beneficial to mothers—certainly it is not something men can feel complacent about. Oakley argues that the contemporary social context of motherhood is "dissatisfying." Social isolation and constant responsibility lead to discontent. Competition with the "demands of housewifery means that to the mother as houseworker the child is something seen as an obstacle to job satisfaction; for the child, the need to juxtapose its demands with those of housework cannot but be experienced as frustrating."[7]

In relation to fathers, Oakley concludes that the tasks men have elected to do—playing with the children, taking them out, putting them to bed—are all too often simply the pleasant and rewarding ones. "This kind of enlargement in the father's role is an unfortunate development," says Oakley, as women "stand to gain little from it but temporary peace to do household chores. . . . At the same time, they lose some of the rewards parenthood offers."

Oakley's observations make intuitive sense. Men take advantage in life in general, so why not in the matter of child care? Lewis's findings confirm this view; he discovered that not only do husbands "undertake less child care," but that they also have "more leisure pursuits than their wives." Lewis adds that one would expect that these "restricted" mothers, these "tied down" mothers, would resent their husbands' freer role, yet his research suggests, on the contrary, that the opposite is the case. On the whole, women *expect* to be more closely tied to the home. Any contribution that their husbands make to family life comes as a pleasant surprise.

In other words, most women are resigned to the fact that men view themselves predominantly as breadwinners and playmates and act accordingly. Because that is what men do in the family, and have done since time immemorial, women come to accept it. A proviso must be added, however: it could be argued that these women are not in fact "pleasurably surprised" if husbands contribute to family life—rather, they are resigned to it, and usually have no choice but to accept the way things are.

Although Lewis's sample is exclusively working class it seems plausible to believe that middle-class men behave in a similar fashion—certainly their longer working day would militate against any greater role than that of playmate. Similarly, one would expect to find their wives resigned, if somewhat grudgingly, to that restricted role. That fathers do not participate centrally in child care seems so clear that it appears indisputable. The idea of the "new man" or the "new father" is a concept designed to fill print space; it is clearly not based in any sense on general reality. There may be individual families and individual fathers who act somewhat differently, but these are in a minority.

This, of course, is not to say that fatherhood is either unimportant or insignificant—in either the father's or the child's life. The vast majority of Lewis's fathers claimed that their child had had a profound influence upon them, or as Lewis puts it, somewhat peculiarly, whatever "a man's previous parental status, parenthood will most likely make him experience a feeling of disequilibrium." In other words, fatherhood brings in its wake new emotions and new responsibilities which alter men's lives. But again it is possible to argue that for the majority of men fatherhood in that sense is merely an interruption—that, unlike women, men's lives are not as changed by fatherhood as women's are by motherhood. Men invariably return quickly to the workplace—the paucity of generous and realistic paternity leave ensures that—and very soon resume their social lives, if they were in fact interrupted at all. The mother, on the other hand, has begun a new life and has become a member of another quite different personal and social universe. The mother will never be the same again.

Of course, most women do not wish to deny their husbands' claims and feelings that fatherhood has "changed their lives" and that their identity is intrinsically linked with their child's. The fact remains, however, that the pattern of men's lives is substantially unchanged as a result of fatherhood. Men want the benefits of children, they want to love and be loved by their children, but they appear to be reluctant to engage in childwork to any great extent. An added irony is that the modern father is "likely to regard himself as more involved in fatherhood than his own father was," yet, as Lewis somewhat gingerly concludes, "the evidence suggests that this may not be wholly true." The cult of child psychology as manifested in magazines and popular books may well prompt the modern father to talk about his role more frequently, but this will not invariably be translated into action. In Lewis's view, fathering in our societies continues to be a "bit of a luxury" which, in the vast majority of circumstances, is an added bonus to the "necessary" function of mothering.

This is exactly what the child has come to expect; mothers do the real mothering—even when they are working full-time—while fathers remain a valuable resource to be called on from time to time. Fathers can be played with and enjoyed; they are unlikely to be as irritable as the mother who has done a day's housework and childwork or carried the double burden of housework and a full-time job—the average full-time working mother works about eighty hours in total for both spheres. And of course the child will reproduce the same pattern in adulthood—what alternative model of parenting do they see? And yet despite the "enlightened" hope of putting an end to this cyclical pattern, Lewis's own subjects appeared reluctant to do so. A major social reorganization would be required to introduce any fundamental change in the balance of responsibility for child care. Lewis's mothers and fathers gave social change of this magnitude a very low priority, when they considered it at all.

What About the Children?

While husband and wife could well be acting out their drama—a tragicomedy, in fact—of maternal and paternal roles, the children are engaged in relationships other than those solely concerned with their parents. From infancy onwards, and with increasing rapidity, children engage in relationships with others—in the main, sisters and brothers, friends, and sometimes "extended kin"—which also have significance for them. Such relationships and their outcomes, of course, also have the effect of adding to or altering the parent-child, child-parent relationship.

Judy Dunn and Carol Kendrick, for example, talk of the "sibling relationship" as one in which doses of "pleasure, affection, hostility, aggression, jealousy, rivalry and frustration are freely and frequently expressed."[8] In fact, if we wish to understand why children differ so much in the affection and hostility that they show towards their siblings, we must take account of the close links between the siblings' relationship and each child's relationship with their parents. Dunn describes these links in a family with two children:

> The patterns are complicated: how a mother behaves with her firstborn daughter before a sibling is born is linked to the extent

of affection and hostility of both children a year later; differences in maternal behaviour towards one child relative to the other are also linked to differences in the siblings' behaviour to each other. We don't know the direction of influence here. It seems plausible that the correlations which the studies reveal reflect causal influence in both directions—that parents affect the sibling relationship *and* that the siblings' relationship influences the parents' behaviour towards both children. The parental relationship appears to be more closely linked to differences in how children behave towards their siblings than are the old favourites age-group and gender.[9]

Here we have moved from talking solely about the importance and influence of the mother, and the maternal role, to that of the influence of parents. The message is clear; what we are seeing is the centrality of mother in the family, in this case the specific influence the mother has in determining how siblings view each other and behave towards each other. Nevertheless, it is crucial not to "blame parents for the hostility between their children." No one, for example, could blame a mother for the intense relationship she has with her firstborn daughter, though it is possible that an overprotective relationship between a mother and a firstborn could lead to an extremely hostile sibling relationship. A child cannot be loved enough. Although the hearts and minds of the young develop and grow in relationships with others, especially their mothers, these hearts and minds remain their own. It would be wrong to underestimate the importance of sibling relationships. Dunn explains that although we cannot safely say how far siblings influence the development of adult personality, we "can say that the power of the relationship lasts far beyond childhood," that it "withstands the separations of time and space, and provides important emotional security for most people in later stages of their lives." Brigid McConville, writing of her own sisters, argues that the "bond" between sisters that is forged in childhood not only endures, but requires hardly any attention in later life in order to flourish.[10] The tie between siblings provides an important buffer against the insecurity of aging and the loss of parents. "Contact with siblings in late adulthood," Dunn says, does not necessarily provide deep intimacy, but it does offer "a sense of contact, belonging and security of attachment to a family."

If relationships with brothers and sisters are valuable, how important are relationships with other nonfamily friends? What can we say about their influence on children's lives?

We all have histories of our favorite friends and the great injuries that go hand in hand with such friendships. Whether it is a question of unrequited love, separation or loss, these friendships are both the essence and the prototype of the bittersweet relationship. The fact that children's friendships can be harmful only serves to underline their importance. Zick Rubin suggests that the behavior of friends ranges from the affectionate to the hostile, and can be intensive or cold.

> Children's close friendships can have undesirable effects as well as desirable ones. Through their relationships with one another, children are likely to learn not only how to get along with others but also how to reject others ("You can't play with us"), to stereotype them ("There's dummy Dwayne"), and to engage in regressive or antisocial behaviour. Intimate friendships give rise not only to self-acceptance, trust, and rapport, but also to insecurity, jealousy, and resentment.[11]

As we know from the evidence of our own lives, friends serve central functions for children that parents do not— they're freely chosen, for a start—and they play a critical role in shaping children's social skills and sense of identity. Clearly a child's experience of, and memory of, friendships, especially early ones, have an impact on later development—including the way they view and behave in relationships of friendship and love. Children's friendships are important quite simply because they add to the child's quality of life. In some quite unusual circumstances such friendships could constitute a child's life—the friendships *are* her life.

Losing friends as a child is part of growing up, a necessary trial run for the marathon of adult life where endless separations take place and indeed have to take place. But the distress of losing childhood friends at the time can never be underestimated—as we all know from our memories of our mother's words of consolation. Rubin's account of children's friendships argues that there is "reason to think" that "girls are more sensitive to the vicissitudes of relationships than boys are," and that it may be for this reason that "women seem to handle separation and loss more effectively than men in adulthood." This is almost self-evident: women tend to be more sensitive than men, are more interested in relationships (and therefore people) than men, and are more comforting at times of distress than men. A woman's life cycle is dominated by motherhood—the most sensitive human condition—whether as a child or as an adult, and girls tend to spend more time with their mothers than their fathers. We could argue that it really is women who should be responsible for "mothering," but this is an issue we will return to later. First we must consider other potential child "caretakers."

Collective and Other Forms of Child Care

We are primarily interested here in child care and day care. Such venerable institutions as "the British nanny" need not concern us, as the traditional nanny has more or less left the planet—"a rather curious way of bringing up children, founded on economic wealth and privilege, which flowered in British society approximately between the years 1850–1939, and then virtually disappeared."[12]

In 1955 Dr. Spock could write that the average day nursery or "baby farm" was detrimental to the baby's first year of life as she needed "a lot of motherly care." For Spock, the attention or affection in the average day nursery was inadequate; in many cases the care there was "matter-of-fact or mechanical rather than warm-hearted." Day care is a critical issue today simply because of the growing number of mothers who work outside of the home (as well as in it) and hence the increased demand for places. The increase in the number of women working has been greater among those *who work part-time.* In the USA more than half of all married women have outside jobs—up from a third in 1950. Women are still doing most of the chores in American households. According to Ann Weber of the University of North Carolina women average thirty hours a week on all household chores and men, a mere four to six hours.

PROPORTIONS OF WOMEN WITH DEPENDENT CHILDREN WORKING FULL AND PART TIME AT DIFFERENT DATES BY AGE OF YOUNGEST CHILD

Age of Youngest Child	Work Status	Date (end December)						
		1949 %	**1954** %	**1959** %	**1964** %	**1969** %	**1974** %	**1979** %
0–4	Full-time	9	6	8	8	8	6	7
	Part-time	5	8	7	10	14	20	19
	All working women	14	14	15	18	22	26	26
5–10	Full-time		21	20	21	23	22	18
	Part-time		19	24	30	33	43	45
	All working women		40	44	51	56	65	63
11–15	Full-time			36	33	31	31	31
	Part-time			30	32	29	42	47
	All working women			66	65	60	73	78

Figures for the earliest dates in each row will be biased because women in these groups are younger on the average for women with youngest child of the given age at the date in question.

Source: J. Martin and C. Roberts, *Women and Employment: A Lifetime Perspective,* HMSO London, p. 12.

Part-time work, however, invariably takes more time than expected; add on traveling time plus arranging and executing child care arrangements and a very different picture of the time involved in "part time" emerges. Alison Clarke-Stewart documents the historical changes that have taken place in this sphere, looks at more recent changes and observes that "for the first time, a majority of school-age children have mothers who work. . . . The fastest growing group in the labor market is mothers of pre-school children, particularly children under three."[13] She singles out five issues pertinent to decisions about day care:[14]

1. It is difficult to know what care arrangements to try to make because a wide variety of types of care are available.

2. There are enormous differences in the quality of care offered in each of these arrangements.

3. Not all types of care and service are available to every mother.

4. "Expert opinion" on the subject of day care is divided and this affects what a mother may or may not do about it.

5. The whole notion of day care "goes against the traditional views of family and child-rearing that our society has espoused for generations, family-orientated views that dominated the upbringing of most of today's working mothers themselves."

This is the context in which such decisions are made; what historical changes brought about the desire to have more day care? Clarke-Stewart suggests a number of reasons:[15]

1. There are obvious economic reasons why some women work— they have to work to "survive."
2. Employed mothers "work because they like their jobs, because they want to have careers, because they want to get out of the house and meet people, have new experiences, avoid boredom, loneliness or frustration."

3. Changes in family composition—for example, family dissolution through divorce, single unmarried mothers—account for part of the increase. Since the turn of the century, there has been a 700 percent rise in the number of marriages ending in divorce.

4. Decreasing availability of other relatives such as grandparents, older siblings and aunts, because of the trend towards smaller families.

5. Changing values, whereby the goal for many parents appears to be personal fulfillment.[16] This frees parents from feeling that exclusive child care is their *duty*.

However, for working mothers (and concerned fathers), the sum total of these changes can only mean added psychological stress—even anxiety or depression. Clarke-Stewart summarizes what is at the heart of the debate over day care, and indeed what concerns mothers, namely the child's social relations.

Opponents fear that children in day care will be deprived of their proper relations with their mothers and will become the pawns of their peers. Advocates claim that children in day care will be appropriately independent of their mothers' apron strings and become more socially competent with their peers.[17]

Opinions, as ever, differ on the issue. Martin Herbert claims that there is no evidence that children of working mothers suffer any adverse effects, providing the substitute care is "good," and as long as a mother feels confident about her reasons for working, and is not paralyzed by nagging doubts. Herbert concludes that

good day care *need not* interfere with *normal* mother-child *bonding*. The use of day nurseries does not *appear* to have any long-term adverse psychological or physical effects . . . [and] . . . On the *whole,* children who go [say] to a *high quality* nursery *may* stand to gain socially and intellectually by becoming more independent and by coming into contact with other children in day care [italics added].[18]

In Herbert's case it is a question of ifs and buts, with talk of "high quality" day care possibly leading to good outcomes, and the evidence appearing to suggest that day care nurseries do not have any long-term adverse psychological or physical effects. Herbert wants to find out what he does in fact find out. Jerome Bruner's extensive study of the subject—*Under Five in Britain*—deals with this very problem of whether day care nurseries are "high quality" or not, concluding that such places vary widely and that it would be wrong "to suppose that all day nurseries or even most day nurseries are of the quality needed." Importantly, Bruner adds a note about a frequently forgotten subject, namely the degree to which substitute parents of all sorts—in this case, the day care nurseries—can and will listen to "problems." Bruner argues that most day care nurseries are "often unable or unwilling to take family problems into account in their care. They serve, rather, as havens away from home for children with troubled families (the chief source of children in such full-day care)." Bruner nonetheless concludes that the "full-time care of children at home in the family in the years preceding school is neither desirable for many families nor, given that fact, is it good for children." It can now "*be taken as certain* that an opportunity to be away from home in a preschool helps the child develop socially, intellectually, and emotionally" (italics added). But if children from troubled families—who presumably have their own problems—are not being listened to in nurseries, how can we be *certain* that such places are good for the child? Bruner himself made the point that the nurseries vary greatly in terms of quality and that we cannot suppose that most day care nurseries are of sufficient quality. His conclusion is particularly instructive:

> The conditions of modern life—its urbanisation, the changed conditions of the family and of women particularly, the altered economic situation—all point to the importance of providing

some community care for children before the age of school entry. It is not self-indulgence that has brought the preschool provisions into existence for children between three and five—or even two and five. Provisions have come into service to serve a need.[19]

The changed "conditions of modern life" to which Bruner refers have been brought about by adults; children did not ask or demand that families be dissolved (not that that in itself is necessarily detrimental to a child who is existing in a negative environment), nor did they ask that the workforce should grow in size and by doing so embrace a larger number of women (and mothers). They certainly did not insist that both parents work in order to amass greater material wealth. This is not a moral argument: the point is that day care was introduced for the adult's benefit; and investigations into whether or not it is helpful or damaging for the child come later. Day care is about adult economics, adult behavior and adult desires. A brief history will make the point.

Children as Displaced Persons

The current day care situation in Britain is not unlike that in the United States; there are historical parallels in day care developments in the two countries. One similarity is in the separate child care streams for rich and poor: nursery schools and day care nurseries. Let us proceed with the case of Britain. The life of the poor in nineteenth-century Britain was not a happy one. It was short, brutish and nasty. Seventy out of every thousand poor children under five years of age did not survive, as a result of crowding, starvation and disease in the cities, and of neglect, drugs, malnutrition and lack of physical or health care in rural areas. Infant mortality was particularly high in families where the mother worked. Children were invariably left unattended or handed to a neighbor. The result, in either case, was unsatisfactory. "Dame schools," in which children were crowded together in ill-ventilated rooms, were little better. Day nurseries were a response to this lack of provision. The first English day nursery opened in London in 1850 with admission dependent on the recommendation of a clergyman or other "respectable person." But fees were high and these types of nurseries (few and far between) were not successful. The development of the free day nurseries—beginning in Manchester in 1871—was more promising. These provided adequate physical care for preschool children, but their numbers were tiny compared with the need. Not until the First World War, when women were needed in munitions factories, was there a major expansion of day care facilities. By 1919, 174 day nurseries had been started, but after the war the number of day nurseries dropped dramatically, not to increase again until the Second World War. Clarke-Stewart takes up their history.

> Beginning in 1940, day nurseries and nursery centres where children could play and learn social skills were set up by the Ministry of Health in areas where there were war evacuees or a shortage of female workers. They were open twelve to fifteen hours a day, and available to working mothers for their pre-school children on payment of a fee. The number of day-care facilities in England and Wales expanded rapidly from 194 full-time centres in 1941 to 1450 in 1944.[20]

As before, however, these also faded away after the war. In peacetime, day care services were to be used only by families with "special needs." From 1945 to the late 1960s, for example, government-subsidized day nurseries declined in number from 1,600 to 466. As in the United States, working mothers had to make private arrangements for alternative child care and the number of private nurseries and registered children's caretakers, in particular, increased.

We know very little about the care that the children of working mothers might receive in their own home—whether from fathers, grandmothers, brothers and sisters, nannies, maids, live-in students, au pairs, friends, neighbors or baby-sitters—probably because this sort of care is a private arrangement. However, legally sanctioned child care has been extensively researched and the findings are not particularly encouraging, especially for the children in question. Bruner, who believes that it is important for preschool children to be away from home, concludes that at present child care "creates problems for at least a third of the children in such care, and for possibly as many as half," and moreover that "the 'quality' of the minder, her degree of concern for children and the setting in which she works, help surprisingly little, though we know that when the setting is less fortunate and the quality of care less good . . . the degree of difficulty increases."[21]

For Bruner, the "heart of the problem" is the discontinuity between the child's home and that of the caretaker's, and the lack of adequate communication between caretaker and mother. He adds that the findings of his research on child care "surely suggest that great caution should be exercised in expanding this form of service," and importantly he questions the extent to which the substitute parent can and does listen to and deal with the child's "problems."

> The incidence of "quiet" or mildly depressed children at the competent and well-placed minders' is too great to overlook and it has been remarked too often to be adventitious. It can be said statistically that the greater the tension and trouble in the home of the child, the more likely is such depressed behaviour to appear at the minder's, whatever her qualifications or setting. The minder does not see herself as a professional in any way, and certainly not as an amateur psychiatrist. Since the minder does not regard it as part of her job to "pry" into the child's home life and since it appears to be the rare mother who shares her personal troubles with her minder, the child's problems are not faced by either.[22]

Bruner sadly concludes that however much we would want it to be otherwise, "the minder's for many children, is not a home away from home . . . but an empty time separated from home."

Clearly, it is important to separate the fact that day care exists from the reasons for its existence; it solves our problems, as adults, just as it did for wartime governments. There is evidence that such substitute care is far from satisfactory for the child concerned. This is not another case for blaming parents, but it is important to know what day care is really about and not conflate that with what we know about its possible effects. It is much more important to know how different industrialized societies pattern their substitute day care, and what lies behind that provision—in other words, what kind of children adults think they are rearing through day care. More sociable, more independent children, or children bereft of full-time motherly love? The brief geographical sketch which follows is based on Clarke-Stewart's survey of the field.

Alternative Visions

Day care as we usually know it began in France, in 1799, when Johann Oberlin, a Protestant minister, was persuaded by his maidservant Louise Sheppler to open the first nursery—in Alsace—as a response to the plight of children left on their own while their mothers worked in the fields. The first *crèche* (infant day nursery) for working mothers was opened in Paris in 1844. Day care for working mothers in France today is provided in *crèches* for infants from six weeks to three years and in *écoles maternelles* for children from three to six years of age. Currently 15 percent of all infants are to be found in *crèches,* while the attendance at the *écoles maternelles* stands at 85 percent. These facilities are neither free nor, in the case of the *crèches,* abundant. There is a sliding scale of fees and for the *crèche* priority is given to single parents or "problem families."

Sweden is well known for the imaginative provision, the quality and rate of both supply and take-up of day care. In Sweden, particularly when compared with Britain and the United States, there is extensive paternity and maternity leave provision, as well as paid leave for parents when a child is sick. Over the years there has been a move, partly successful, to reduce the length of the working week for both parents. The day care centers, *daghems,* provide "high quality" care for children aged from six months to seven years. Even in Sweden, however, where the proportion of working women is high (over 65 percent), the demand for places far exceeds the supply.

The case of the Soviet Union is instructive in that it is the example *par excellence* of children being placed in day care because the state demands (and needs) it and the economy relies upon it. This collective substitute care is considered to be appropriate for a society which rests on a belief in collectivism. As it is essential for the Russian economy that mothers work, the Russians have created the most extensive program of child care provision ever known. Central to this program are the *yashi-sads* (nurseries and kindergartens), although children are still more likely to be cared for by a *babushka* (grandmother) in their infancy. Lacking a *babushka,* the state nurseries are available for babies from six weeks of age onwards. In Moscow alone there are about three thousand *yashi-sads,* while an estimated thirteen million Soviet children are in full-time care. The People's Republic of China similarly has an extensive network of nurseries, usually factory-based, but invariably the system is more casual, as is clear from the widespread use of the Chinese "auntie" in child care.

However, the example most often used in discussions of the purpose of substitute care is that of the *kibbutzim* in Israel— despite the fact that only 3 percent of the population live in in *kibbutzim*. This collective style of living has not arisen solely because mothers have chosen to work; rather, it is part and parcel of a communal ideology. Bruno Bettelheim, in *The Children of the Dream*, describes a typical "children's house":

> Kibbutz children live from birth (usually from the fourth day after delivery) with their age group, not at home with their families. That is, they are raised as a group, in separate children's houses, by members of the community assigned to the task. Usually the children's houses are built in a cluster, set off from the other kibbutz structures.
>
> . . . But usually the newborn who enters the infants' house is placed in a room with four to six cribs. The house has four or five such rooms and contains some twenty or more infants.
>
> Each group of infants has one metapelet who is essentially in charge of that room, or else in charge of two rooms, but with a helper. In most kibbutzim for the first six months of his life the infant does not leave the infants' house, though his mother nurses him there and his father may visit. . . . If an infant, or later an older child, is sick and does not require hospitalization, he does not go to school but remains in his crib or bed in the children's house and is nursed by the metapelet. Thus sickness does not alter the child care arrangements.
>
> When the infant is anywhere between one and two years old, he leaves the infants' house and moves to the toddlers' house. There a group of about six children are cared for by one metapelet. Each toddlers' house contains two or more such groups who share a common playroom and dining room.[23]

And so it goes on up the age range. Bettelheim claims that there are "no neglected children in the kibbutz, none whose physical needs in sickness and health are not well taken care of, none who could not learn in school because they had no decent place to sleep, or enough to eat, and there is no child who fails because of too much pressure to compete and perform." The *kibbutz* can offer these facilities, he adds, "precisely because, in return for its protection, its members grant it so much control of their lives." This communal or collective substitute care is, understandably, reflected in the children's relationships. *Kibbutz* children form strong, positive relationships with their mothers, siblings and friends, just like children in more traditional family arrangements, but their emotions—both positive and negative—in those relationships are more moderate and not so focused on single individuals. Rather, they spread their affection across a larger number of people and have less deeply intimate relations with any one person.

Different people hold different views on both the efficacy and the desirability of the personality change desired by the *kibbutzim*. Jonathan Gathorne-Hardy is convinced that the "children of the dream" showed that it was possible to "create a *radical* new personality for a people in a generation"—in their case, a metamorphosis from "over-emotional, property hungry, tight, ghetto Jews to under-emotional non-property-owning, open, rational Israeli farmers." Once again his conclusion is instructive.

> There may be something to question or regret about a kibbutz upbringing, but there can be no doubt at all that it produces adults infinitely more stable, happier, able to live fuller lives than, say, many children from broken families in the slums of Glasgow or New York or children brought up among the intense conflicts of a disintegrating middle-class family in an isolating suburb. If there are really women who wish to have children and only to look after them one or two hours a day while they pursue other goals, then there exists a perfectly sound model for them to copy.[24]

Exactly. Forms and types of day care are models. They are adult constructions designed to enable adults to do things other than full-time parenting at home and, in the case of the *kibbutzim*, to create particular kinds of people. Only later, in retrospect, do we decide to evaluate such care. The trouble with day care in the United States and Britain is that we have neither made the day care uniform in quality, nor decided what kind of children such day care will produce. And even if we decided that what we hoped for from such care was a degree of collectivism or communality in the child's attitudes and per- sonality, or an "under-emotional" child, we have not made our other institutions of socialization compatible with such aims. The "normal family" tends to aim for individualism and self- interest, as do the educational and occupational systems.

I will not be looking at those substitutes who are brought into play when young children go into state "care" because of disasters at home—foster parents, adoptive parents or forms of children's homes—as I intend to argue along more general lines. However, despite our endless self-congratulations about our child-rearing practices, growing numbers of children enter state "care." Take the example of Britain: despite the rhetoric of prevention and the passing of two major pieces of legislation, the Children and Young Persons Acts of 1963 and 1969, part of whose aim was to divert children from care, the number and proportion of children in care has risen, almost without interruption, for twenty years. The statistics for England and Wales for 1962 show a total of 63,500 children in care, or 5.1 percent per 1,000 of the eligible population under eighteen years of age. The corresponding figures for 1981 were a total of 97,000 in care or a rate of 7.6 percent. To take the year ending in March 1983, over 34,000 children came into state care (in England and Wales). The circumstances surrounding the placement in care, and the care experience itself, can never be positive, and are invariably tragic, as one young girl explained (quoted in Stein and Carey):

> I remember the social worker coming to the school with my two brothers in the car and picking me up. I never got the chance to say goodbye to the woman who had been fostering us. We went straight from school and took my brothers to one home and then I went straight from there to a home in another place, a foster home, and I never saw my brothers again until I

was ten years old. When I was taken away from the foster parents I had, for ill-treatment, I went to another home again and then I got contact again with my two brothers; and when I was about thirteen years old I was asking about my parents because I'd never seen them in all that time. I found out my father had died and they'd never heard about it, so when I was about thirteen years old the social worker arranged a meeting with my mother, at the home I was at. We'd all gone out one day with the other staff and other children to a playing field and they brought my mum and my sister to the playing field, and that was the first time I'd seen my mum for about eleven years. That was a very upsetting time.

I didn't understand a thing until I got to be older and then I could understand. . . . It wasn't until I went to the home that I had anything explained to me and was told why things were happening and what was happening; when I was younger I could never understand why we had to be separated, me and my brothers.[25]

Interestingly enough, the same researchers found that many children valued children's homes because they were homes. There may well have been restrictions, the exercise of authority and variable staff, but the fact that they were homes helped. We may in time see a reversal from the current ideology—for that is what it is—whereby children are kept out as much as possible from residential forms of care, and a return again to homes. Perhaps we should not dismiss residential homes per se. No two institutions are the same, just as the effects on development, good or bad, vary from one institution to another. Instead of merely rejecting the idea of a residential home, it should not, as Jack and Barbara Tizard argue, be "impossible to carry out studies designed explicitly to measure the 'emotional climate' of institutions serving the needs of young children, to explore the organisational arrangements which facilitate different types of staff-child interaction, and to assess the effect of these upon the children's emotional well-being."[26]

In terms of foster care and adoption we know both a lot and a little. We know, intuitively as well as academically, that adopted children and adoptive parents have a better chance with each other if they commence their relationship earlier rather than later. But in the case of foster care we also know there are numerous and invariable breakdowns in relationships. Where the child in a foster care arrangement is old enough to know the purpose of the relationship, it is perhaps surprising that so few actually break down—what can be more unsettling and frustrating for a child than to know that she is in a period of transition, she is a displaced person, she is not where she belongs. However, no one can deny the positive value of "good" and supportive foster care such as James and Joyce Robertson have amply demonstrated.

The move to a more permanent arrangement, notably adoption, is also fraught with difficulties. Quite simply, the "route to permanence must be unique to each child." As June Thoburn, Anne Murdoch and Alison O'Brien point out in their study of the possibilities for permanence, for "each and every case the 'chemistry'—the relationship between the child and those he loved in the past, and those he may come to love in the future—will be different."[27]

Polly Toynbee's *Lost Children,* an account of British adopted children and their new rights as formalized in the 1975 Children's Act, also offers new insights into an old problem. The search by adopted children for their "real" or "natural" mothers has for a long time been a literary and dramatic theme, but since the passing of the legislation in question it has become a part of reality for many.

> Let no one doubt the desperate urgency some adopted and lost children feel in their search for their parents. It can become a grinding obsession, a full-time waking and sleeping need that drives them on beyond the limits of reason. . . .
> Tom O'Mara always intended to set out to look for his mother, but the need did not take hold of him until he was in his

forties, and very happily married with two children. Once he decided to embark on the search, then nothing on earth could hold him back. He worked at it every spare moment, he thought of nothing else night and day. He spent all his spare money on it. Every rebuff, every set-back only spurred him on further. And when the final disaster struck and his mother refused to meet him, even that did not stop his determination to know his family. He laid siege to her. He contacted those around her, and he watched her secretly, unknown and unrecognized.[28]

This is not surprising, partly because our culture places stress on family values and family relationships. To say that one is adopted will not necessarily result in stigma, but it will ensure that the person in question is viewed differently—as somewhat abnormal. Toynbee offers another similar explanation: "Time and again these adopted people reiterated the same theme. Different people brought up in different families and circumstances, and yet almost all were emphatic about one thing—blood is important. Kith, and kin, clan and ancestors matter." Since every human civilization has held family and blood kinship in high esteem, it should be no surprise that adopted children often feel that they have been "denied a part of their natural birthright." Toynbee is not in any sense using a biological argument, but rather a sociological one, for she adds that in the past it was not common practice to tell all adopted children of their true origins, as it has been for at least a generation, and suggests that if "adopted children never knew that those who brought them up were not their real parents, perhaps none of this would arise." Toynbee doubts that many people would claim any special bond between a mother and her child, if neither one of them knew of the relationship.

In *Divorce Matters,* Jacqueline Burgoyne, Roger Ormrod and Martin Richards make a similar point in relation to the separations created by divorce. They claim that parents are important because they *are* parents, not merely because of their domestic or child care responsibilities. This is "not an argument for the importance of blood ties but rather for the way in which parenthood is socially constructed within our society." In other words, children grow up assuming their parents to be important to them, not least because that is the assumption that everyone around them makes. From the child's point of view this does not change at divorce; the ties of parenthood can stretch across distance and are maintained even if meetings are brief and infrequent. Burgoyne, Ormrod and Richards importantly and sensibly add that the fact that "a child has moved into a new household, perhaps with a potential step-parent, does not mean that their need to remain in some kind of contact with the absent parent ceases."

In an interesting conclusion to her book Toynbee asks, "Why does the first mother have to be cut out of the child's life so absolutely?," particularly as cutting a child away from its mother in this way is

> now profoundly out of keeping with all other aspects of child care. The first mother is seen as such a threat that she must, on an adoption order being made, disappear for ever and never know the destination or the destiny of her baby. The reason, I suspect, is that adoption is still seen as a kind of unconscious deception. The adopters are the ewes who might reject the child unless they are allowed to pretend to themselves that this child is indeed their own.[29]

5

What Happens When Things Go Wrong?

I was wondering whether in the new *Oxford Dictionary of Quotations* I was going to be lumbered with "They fuck you up, your mum and dad." I had it on good authority that this is what they'd been told is my best-known line, and I wouldn't want it thought that I didn't like my parents. I did like them. But at the same time they were rather awkward people and they were never very good at being happy. And these things rub off.

Philip Larkin, *Required Writing*

ASKING why couples break up their relationships and cause each other so much pain is about as easy to answer as to why they fell in "love"—or at least decided to make such a commitment to each other—in the first place. Without even using the term "love" no one can be *precise* as to why individuals decide to put themselves at the mercy of and in the service of someone else. Similarly, it is hard to know why exactly such relationships stop working: it is often a question of incompatible sexual relations; financial strain can be a contributory factor; the two personalities may have developed unequally and are unbalanced; their different needs may have changed over time and may be met more fully by someone other than the original partner; they could well be bored with each other's company;

one partner could feel dissatisfied while the other could still be in a state of satisfaction; one partner might simply want out for all sorts of reasons. All of these reasons take us so far, but why the moment, why the finality, we cannot know. When children are involved they make a decision to leave or to part all the more difficult and at the same time could well be a contributory factor in the first place—the birth of a child may significantly alter sexual relations—indeed, sexual pleasure—between a couple; an extra mouth or two to feed costs money that might be in short supply; the child may create new feelings, alter personalities, produce new allegiances. How does marital separation and divorce affect the children? Have views changed on this over the years?

Divorce Matters

Although we may like to think, in those moments when we believe we know more and are more realistic than our parents or our parents' parents, that the current climate is more "enlightened" about the effects of divorce, it is not necessarily so. For a start, not everyone in our parents' generation believed that couples ought to stay together "for the sake of the children." When divorce was a much rarer occurrence than today, people not only viewed it as abhorrent but also realized that if people were taking such a drastic step there must be something seriously wrong with the relationship. Dr. Spock, writing in 1955 on the subject of marital separation, wrote that it was important to let children see "that even though the parents separate, the children will still belong to both and will always be able to see both regularly . . . that neither parent is the good one nor the bad one. This is the hardest rule for the parents to live by."[1]

Ann Mitchell's research into the lives of children living

through divorce also offers support to those who, like myself, do not quite believe children are as *adaptable* as we would wish them to be in such circumstances. As Mitchell puts it, after divorce or separation we should be fully "conscious of the bewilderment and unhappiness children may be experiencing, especially if they do not show their feelings."[2] In Mitchell's sample of divorced families very few parents had explained adequately the reasons for their family splitting up, and two-thirds of them said that they had given their children no explanation at all. Not surprisingly then, many of the children concerned were bewildered, not knowing whether the separation was to be temporary or permanent, and moreover not believing their parents' arguments to be sufficient reason for breaking up their family. If the reason was obvious to the parents, the children did not necessarily agree.

Although we like to believe that children are adaptable in these circumstances, parents themselves are also less adaptable than we might like to think. Divorce is on the increase, but like the mythical past when we believed it was all stigma and no acceptance, today divorce is as much surrounded by stigma as it is understood and accepted. It remains a private affair. Mitchell notes that

> for parents and children, separation and divorce may be seen as private or shameful, leading to a reluctance to acknowledge the need for help. There is also an underlying ambivalence among parents and especially among children about whether separation is the best solution to an unhappy marriage. Parents make the decisions and children seldom have an opportunity to make their views known.[3]

It is not therefore surprising to learn that only a few of Mitchell's parents had given any thought to the effect of the separation on their children. The parents had probably been too preoccupied with their own feelings to understand their children's needs, while some children had deliberately and successfully concealed their feelings from their parents and appeared to have given emotional support to their parents. Sadly, half of the children described by Mitchell did not remember any parental conflict before separation, and a majority thought their family life had been happy. One in six—five years later—had continued to long for reconciliation.

Burgoyne, Ormrod and Richards pursue the psychological consequences a little further in their book, *Divorce Matters*. They are less pessimistic in their views. Statistically they claim that two-thirds of divorces in Britain involve marriages with children and about one-third of these children are under five at the time. But statistics conceal more than they reveal. Divorces vary, children vary. Children react differently to these events. Not only does it make an enormous difference whether they are five or fifteen, but much depends on the kind of child they are, how they deal with difficulties, the kind of relationships they have with their parents and their own expectations of family life. There is not a single set of reactions of children to divorce, but there are some common themes—both features of the situation and children's reactions—which occur frequently and thus allow us to talk about divorce and children in general.

One of the first signs that children may be affected by an impending or actual separation is their fear of being alone. Echoing Bowlby, the authors add that behavior of this kind by the child is a clear indication that he or she is anxious that their remaining parent may disappear, an understandable fear if you consider marital separation from a child's point of view.

Young children generally believe that social relationships, especially those with their parents and other family members, are everlasting. These people are the constant feature in a child's life and the base from which a child looks out to the rest of the world. Separation and divorce are deeply disturbing because they demonstrate to a child that social relationships can end, even those as fundamental as the ones they have with their own parents or the bond between their parents.[4]

Burgoyne, Ormrod and Richards reiterate Mitchell's point that despite what some parents might prefer to believe, it is rare for a child to welcome a separation. They may welcome the "end of bickering and strife, or violence if this has occurred, but very few children want their parents to part." Children do not choose a parental separation; rather, as Mitchell has also argued, it is imposed on them. Again with echoes of Bowlby they suggest that to make all this worse, it is imposed by the "very people on whom a child depends most and to whom they look for protection of their interests." This adds, of course, to a child's sense of abandonment together with the disturbing feelings of powerlessness.

In the calamity of divorce, children may regress to earlier patterns of behavior that they had given up as they got older— which is not surprising if it is true that what they are really looking for is protection. It is often said that children feel guilty and responsible for their parents' divorce, believing that something they had done had driven their parents apart. While guilt is common, this is not usually its origin, as Burgoyne, Ormrod and Richards point out:

In fact, there is evidence that such feelings of responsibility seem to be confined to very young children and even then appear to be quite rare. The widespread belief that children bear such feelings of responsibility despite evidence to the contrary is perhaps an indication of what adults would prefer to believe about the origins of their child's unhappiness. If a child is obviously upset by what is going on, it is perhaps easier to accept that the upset is due to a childish misunderstanding of the cause of what is happening—the inappropriate guilt—than to accept that it is directly caused by the parents making a decision that the child does not want and may continue to resent deeply for some time afterwards.[5]

The notion of a child acting on the basis of real events in her life rather than misunderstandings or indeed fantasies is in keeping with Bowlby's views. However, the authors believe, contrary to Bowlby and others, for example, that if there are effects on the child from such separations, they are either short-lived or if long-term only slight.

The overt distress of children when their parents separate and eventually divorce is generally short-lived, they argue, although it may last for a matter of months or a year, after which it will gradually subside. The time this takes clearly depends very much on what happens after the divorce and the quality of the children's relationships with both parents. Basically, the better their relationships with their parents, the less marked the distress will be and the shorter its duration. In terms of access, for example, the pattern that this takes immediately after separation usually sets the pattern for the future. As Judith Wallerstein and Joan Kelly have found, the sooner and the more frequently that children have access, the more likely they are to continue to keep in touch with the absent parent. Those who had no access in the beginning found difficulties in restoring broken relationships and then in maintaining them.[6]

Burgoyne, Ormrod and Richards are convinced that any effects that do persist over the years are slight. However, while research into long-term effects is difficult to carry out, there are long-term possibilities—an "increased likelihood of children who have experienced their parents' divorce eventually divorcing themselves" and the finding that "juvenile delinquency, and depression and other psychological difficulties may be more common later in life."[7] Putting to one side the fact that divorced children are quite likely to live through some financial insecurity and social stigma, they clearly have also had their sense of security crushed—and hence their own self-esteem—and in addition face a new role model to imitate. It is not surprising that children who have experienced a divorce are more likely to be involved in a divorce themselves. It does not always happen, but it is not unreasonable for the child of a divorce to search for some kind of "perfect partner," someone who will "never leave," someone who is reliable, someone who is "safe," someone who will "protect." Such allegiances may not be realistic and could ultimately lead to divorce. On the other hand, perhaps becoming divorced themselves may be the only way they can demonstrate anger to parents or the only way they can share something with a parent.

What are these families or households that are created and destroyed?

The Family: Haven or Horror Story?

Leo Tolstoy in *Anna Karenina* made his famous observation that while "all happy families resemble one another, each unhappy family is unhappy in its own way," while Anthony Hope, in *The Prisoner of Zenda,* wrote that "good families are generally worse than any others." They are both right, and the truth probably lies somewhere in between. In other words, the family is an area of human life besieged by ideology and preconceived if contradictory notions.

Bowlby, as we have seen, believed the family to be the most suitable environment in which the mother–child relationship could flourish, although he recognized at the same time that unhealthy families did exist and moreover that families were subject to economic pressure and strain. Relationships are also at the center of R. D. Laing's account (see, for example, *The Politics of the Family*) of family life where he observes that the close-knit emotional tangles of the nuclear "family nexus" can lead to all sorts of disturbances; indeed, in extreme cases to schizophrenia. This is the logical outcome of Laing's model of the nuclear family in which each member "attempts to regulate the inner life of the other in order to preserve his own. "[8] As Michele Barrett and Mary McIntosh argue, from Laing's accounts of the families of his schizophrenic patients, it is "not hard to see how the tight intimacy of nuclear family life may cause acute problems for family members, even when the solutions they seek are less dramatic than schizophrenia."[9] Barrett and McIntosh write as feminists and aim for a more communal ethic of child-rearing as a solution to what they see as the oppression of family life. In a similar vein Oakley claims that the modern nuclear family cannot satisfy women's and hence mothers' needs (and presumably also their children's).

What the gender-differentiated nuclear family produces is two classes of people—men and women—who cannot satisfy one another's relational needs. Men want their relational needs to be satisfied in a heterosexual connection with women, while women look, throughout their lives, and in one way or another, back to the original symbiosis of the mother-child relationship. When one compares contemporary industrial society with other non-industrialized cultures, the absence of patterned cooperation and friendship between adult women is one of the most striking differences. Women in many other cultures look to each other for daily help and support and emotional gratification. They did so in our own society before industrialization and before the rise of the nuclear family ethic, according to which the love between man and woman is every woman's salvation. In fact, of course, the promise of this love is every woman's downfall, for as long as women believe in *men* as their saviours they will not be able to find themselves. The nuclear family provides women with only one culturally accepted solution to their own gendered, family-produced needs for intense primary relationships: and that is to invest their emotional futures in their children.[10]

Oakley may well be too rhetorical in her views as women *have* come to depend on each other in the past two decades— hence the reality of "sisterhood," let alone the practical cooperation between women we see in the world of playgroups, for example. Nevertheless, there is a profound and depressing truth to her argument.

Certainly the family has changed since the 1940s and 1950s, the period in which Bowlby was writing, and against this background "mothering" may not be such a valuable experience; it is also probably more difficult to carry out. This is an argument we will return to in a later chapter; here I want to consider a number of more immediately relevant points. First, the changes that have taken place; and then the changes that have *not* occurred.

Swings and Roundabouts

Marriage in Britain has never been as popular as it is today. In 1951, 15 percent of women aged between forty and forty-five had never married, but the corresponding figures for 1971 and 1985 were 8 percent and 5 percent respectively; cohabitation is more often a prelude to marriage than people might imagine, and these days one-fifth of all couples cohabit prior to marriage, while two-thirds of all couples cohabit prior to remarriage; but women are marrying later on in life, with the figures for 1972 showing that one-third of first-time marriages were teenagers compared with one-fifth in 1982. Divorce rates have risen massively since the 1940s. Of those children born in 1946, it is estimated that 6 percent had experienced divorce of their parents while still children. For those children born in the 1980s, however, 20 percent are likely to experience the divorce of their parents while still children. Remarriage has increased also, although the rate is about three or four times higher for men than for women. In 1972, 20 percent of marriages were remarriages for one or both partners, and by 1985 this had risen to 35 percent. Some 90 percent of married couples have children, but family size is declining. Illegitimate births have increased in the last decade from 48,000 (6 percent of all live births) in 1961 to 81,000 (13 percent of all live births) in 1981. And since 1981 the number of illegitimate births has increased greatly, in 1986 comprising 20 percent of all births.

In the period in which Bowlby has been attempting to convey his message of the importance of family life (with the centrality of the mother-child relationship), the desire for family life (or at least marriage) has not waned, but people's ability to keep families together once they have been established appears to have diminished. In Bowlby's writings the concept of the "normal" family was constantly used to mean a small nuclear unit with an extended network at not too great a geographical distance, but as Jon Bernardes shows in his analysis of census statistics, the "normal family" is so rare as to render the "whole idea of a single central type of 'family' quite redundant."[11] This is often used as if it meant that a "normal family" has never existed, which may be partly true, but nonetheless ignores the rise in the number of one-parent families.

Another change that is much talked about is the demise of the extended family with the ever-increasing development of industrialization and the subsequent processes of geographical (and social) mobility. Vance Packard, for example, in his much underrated *A Nation of Strangers,* documents the experience of geographical mobility in the United States, and points out that the average American moves about fourteen times in his or her lifetime and that about "40 million Americans change their home address at least once a year." According to Packard, the consequence is a substantial "increase of inhabitants suffering a loss of identity and continuity"; these losses all "contribute to a deteriorating sense of well-being, both for individuals and for society." Packard argues that loneliness is increasingly prevalent as more and more people live alone or in smaller families. As in Britain, people in the United States are marrying later, having fewer children, divorcing more often and moving greater distances away from "home." He concludes that "we are fast becoming not only a nation of strangers, but a nation of lonely strangers at that."[12] On the virtues of the extended family—the combination of families of origin and marriage—Michael Young and Peter Willmott, in their account of Bethnal Green, in East London, recounted how such an arrangement strengthened, among other things, the mother-daughter relationship.

> The woman is not cut off from her daughter by marriage. While in one way she has lost her to her new son-in-law, in another way she has recovered her as a daughter. Previous crises in the life of the family, beginning of school and start of work, have withdrawn daughter as well as son from the mother's home. . . . But when she marries, and even more when she leaves work to have children, she returns to the woman's world, and to her mother. Marriage divides the sexes into their distinctive roles, and so strengthens the relationship between the daughter and the mother who has been through it all before. . . . The daughter continues to live near her mother. She is a member of her extended family. She receives advice and support from her in the great personal crises and on the small domestic occasions. They share so much and give such help to each other because, in their women's world, they have the same functions of caring, for home and bringing up children.[13]

This portrait of working-class family life could well have been written by Bowlby himself, so supportive is he in his own writings of the role that the grandmother, especially the maternal one, can play in the life of a child and her mother. But it would be wrong to demarcate clearly between the two different forms of the modern family—the extended and nuclear—as the picture is not quite as clear as it might appear at first glance, and there are other changes to the family and its dimensions which are instructive to our discussion.

To begin with, the evidence is both uncertain and misleading. Peter Laslett, who paints an extremely vivid picture of the extended family in England in the seventeenth century, is nonetheless uncertain about the relevant evidence.

> It seems very likely from such evidence as has been surveyed that the child of peasant parents was brought up with a bevy of other children, caressed and attended to by a knot of other mothers and other adults, too, as is known to be the situation in many "primitive" societies today, rather than being nurtured in the privacy of the cottage, the shack or the boarded-off rooms which the family inhabited. A little boy or a little girl with such a plurality of parental figures would seem likely to have felt the deprivation and the sudden change rather less keenly than one who, like the children in the supposedly isolated cell of the late-twentieth-century conjugal family, had been exclusively tied to two parents, and especially to the mother.[14]

However, in a footnote Laslett points out that the sources "cannot be said to be certain" on the matter. Similarly, Adam Kuper argues that one lesson from historians of the family is that "the past was rather like the present," that the modern nuclear family is less isolated than had been supposed, and that the preindustrial nuclear family was more "independent of encompassing institutions." Kuper adds that comparative anthropology also suggests that there is little cross-cultural variation—"independent nuclear families crop up among Eskimos and African pastoralists, Chinese and Indian villagers, and even in the Israeli kibbutz." He suggests also that the range of historical variation is surprisingly limited and that "unexpected parallels throw into relief the continuities of form." Kuper elaborates:

> The Victorians did not go in much for divorce, but their marriages were also extremely unstable because women died with distressing regularity in childbirth. Many men buried two,

three or even four wives. Nor did respectable Victorians fancy "living together," but common-law marriages were quite normal among industrial workers.[15]

Kuper suggests that the family is "more robust" than had once been suspected: perhaps we are now seeing a return to strictly traditional forms—hence the current high remarriage rate?—despite the changes that have occurred especially since the middle 1960s. In conclusion, Kuper argues that it is wrong to underestimate the changes that have occurred in the last twenty years, perhaps the most dramatic being the "wide dissemination of the contraceptive pill, which for the first time in history provided women with reliable, independent control of their own fertility." Nevertheless, he adds, "rumours of revolution are probably overdone." Concern about AIDS, of course, may favor monogamy once more.

Generally speaking, the nuclear family in the industrialized nations seems to flourish as strongly as ever, occasionally supported by a more extended network. Divorce continues to rise, but so does remarriage. But it is important—particularly when considering Britain and the United States—to remember the role that consumer capitalism plays in the lives of family members and indeed the effect it has on producing all manner of tensions and strains. Christopher Lasch, who has always been a staunch supporter of the family, offers such an analysis in *The Minimal Self,* appropriately enough subtitled *Psychic Survival in Troubled Times.*

Lasch begins his analysis by stating that the modern family as we know it is the product of nineteenth-century "egalitarian ideology, consumer capitalism, and therapeutic intervention," resulting in "weakened parental authority." In the twentieth century, according to Lasch, the

advertising industry further weakened parental authority by glorifying youth. Advertising, like the service professions, insisted that parents owed their children the best of everything while insisting that they had only a rudimentary understanding of children's needs. . . . In general, the culture of consumption promoted the idea that women and children should have equal access, as consumers, to an ever-increasing abundance of commodities. At the same time, it reduced the father's role in the family to that of a breadwinner.[16]

No one can deny the additional pressures such raised expectations have placed upon an already vulnerable institution, the family, particularly those families which were both encouraged to raise their material "standards" while at the same time denied access (by inequality and poverty) to those resources which would enable them to reach such "standards." Lasch argues that such changes hardly add up to a "matriarchal" revolution, as antifeminists have sometimes claimed, nor did they even create a child-centered family in the sense of giving children a veto over their parents' authority. They may have gone some way towards freeing women and children from patriarchal despotism in the home, but they did very little to strengthen their position in the outside world. Lasch continues with a much neglected theme in the current writing on the family in crisis:

In the case of children, the decline of parental supervision— however oppressive parental supervision may have been in the old days—turned out to be a dubious blessing. Not only did it deprive children of parental guidance, it went hand in hand with the second pattern of long-term historical change, the partial replacement of the family by other socializing agencies, which exposed children to new forms of manipulation, sexual seduction, and outright sexual exploitation.[17]

There is a great deal of cant in any discussion on parental guidance. Our Western industrialized nations must be historically unique in deriding old age. Experience (which comes with age) is totally undervalued, but in an area like the rearing of children, where and how can one learn about it except by experience? Moreover, as Lasch argues, agencies of social control such as schools, which are concerned with controlling both the bodies and the minds of children—and glorifying them at the same time—have filled the void. This is hardly progressive.

Lasch continues his analysis by arguing that to confront children with information for which they are emotionally unprepared undermines the child's confidence in adult authority: "The child comes to feel that he and they [adults] live in different spiritual worlds." Lasch believes that the neglect of children is part of the broader pattern of neglect that includes the "reckless exploitation of natural resources, the pollution of the air and water, and the willingness to risk 'limited' nuclear wars as an instrument of national policy."

For Lasch, children have paid a "heavy price for the new freedom enjoyed by adults"—the freedoms gained by allowing other institutions space to rear children. In particular, he finds the most disturbing sign of the "prevailing indifference to the needs of children," the growing inclination to "exploit them sexually in movies and advertising, perhaps also in actual practice." His conclusions are somber:

> . . . the feeling that adults are helpless in dealing with children, powerless to offer them a sheltered space to grow up in or protect them from the devastating impact of the adult world, and therefore not responsible for failing to protect them or even for exploiting them in ways that make nineteenth-century child labor look almost benign by comparison.[18]

Lasch's arguments are of an extremely general and sweeping nature, but nevertheless cogent enough to be coherent, and convincing enough to be plausible. The escalating divorce rate, the increasing rate of remarriage, the escalating child abuse rate all add up to a portrait of despair. This is not to say that there aren't "happy families" everywhere, because there are people who find happiness in this way, but even those people are aware of what is happening around them and prone to such possibilities.

There is certainly no doubt that individuals continue to search for the family life they believe will lead them to some form of personal fulfillment. As Jacqueline Burgoyne, in her study of stepfamilies—of which, in the United States, thirteen hundred are formed every day—interestingly notes, such desires do exist and are inevitably tied to material expectations and to notions of material happiness.

> The notion of a "normal family" was very important for the remarried parents we studied and their decision to remarry was frequently explained as the result of their desire to recreate an "ordinary family life" for themselves and their children. Their detailed descriptions of the way earlier marriages had ended, their periods alone as single parents, as well as the whole process of family reconstitution, provided a vivid demonstration of the ways in which the emotional and material aspects of family life are interwoven.[19]

Where Did Our Love Go?

If it is difficult to know what causes marriages to gel and what splits them asunder, it is equally difficult to understand the nature of the love we are supposed to give to each other and our children. I say "supposed" because despite contemporary cynicism, we know that that is possibly the only way the majority of us can find fulfillment—not all of us can be (or desire to be) power-brokers or solitary artists. Bowlby, of course, is unashamed about it, and called one of his books after such a quality. As a concept, "love" is abhorrent to modern scientific thinking, as it cannot be measured, and what cannot be measured—according to such thinking—does not exist.

What is love—in this case mother love, because that is the prototype of all love (whether to give or to receive) and the most important of all because it is where human life grows and develops?

Freud argued that love is similar to a psychotic state, while physiologist Dorothy Tennov talks about it being initiated in the limbic or primitive part of the brain, which "governs our reptilian, ritualistic functions." Love is often considered to be a chemical reaction, in which the brain produces phenylethylamine, equivalent to, say, an amphetamine "high." The same theory argues conversely that the spurned lover (and hence the spurned brain) experiences drug-withdrawal symptoms, causing severe "craving for chocolate, which contains phenylethylamine."[20] Certainly we think love is important, yet no one believes there is much to be learned about love. What is clear, though, is that for the majority of us in the industrialized nations love equals romantic love.

"Romantic love" sweeps all before it and is often expressed in terms of "sickness" and sadness: like parting, it is sweet sorrow. Romantic love is the ideal of pure, unfulfilled love that is celebrated by the poets and acted out in so many of the great dramas—Romeo and Juliet, Tristan and Isolde, Heloïse and Abelard are classic examples. Romantic love has its own mythology—persuasive but impossible to prove or disprove—in which love occurs at first sight; love conquers all; women are more romantic than men; and for each person there is one predestined true love. Maurice Lamm observes that "pure romantic love is applied only to love outside marriage. While it is true that romantic love did become a sort of precondition to married life at the end of the sixteenth century, its outlook could never be suitably adapted to this state."[21]

Romantic love can only be defined as a strong emotional attachment to another person with a tendency towards idealization and a marked physical attraction. Unfortunately, this idealization of the other person, the loved one, requires a psychological, physical or social remoteness if it is to be maintained. Hence the inherent paradox: romantic love desires intimacy, but at the very moment of intimacy, love evaporates. Romantic love foists upon the world the illusion that a partner must be capable of providing a life of continuous ecstasy. Unfortunately, passion has a marked tendency to spend itself quickly. Romantic love, by holding out the possibility of perpetual passion, raises unrealistic expectations. When no passion is experienced and the embers have cooled, many think that their marriage has failed—because one partner, or indeed both, is miserable. Most of marriage's ills could perhaps be traced to the faulty selection of a spouse, but so fundamental is the notion of romantic love to our lives that we do not realize how small a part of humankind through history has shared it.

But just as there are social cycles of deprivation based on the family experiences of our childhood, similarly spouse selection can only have its origins in the way that as children we view our parents' relationships and our individual relationships with both father and mother. Which leads us back to the nature of mother love and its consequences.

So although the notion of romantic love is what we can term the "dominant ideology," it has been criticized as a poor basis for long-term relationships, including marriage. Erich Fromm, in his influential *The Art of Loving,* poses the question "Is love an art?" If it is, it requires knowledge and effort. Or is love a pleasant sensation, experienced as a matter of chance, something one "falls into" if one is lucky? Fromm believes the former while he considers that the majority of people believe in the latter. He points to three sets of problems. First, most people see the problem of love primarily as that of being loved rather than that of loving, of one's capacity to love. Secondly, is the related assumption that the problem of love is the problem of an object, not the problem of a faculty. Fromm considers that people think that to love is simple, but that to find the right object to love, or to be loved by, is difficult. He argues that contemporary Western culture is based on the appetite for buying, on the idea of a mutually favorable exchange. "Attractive" people are sought from the personality market—"what specifically makes a person attractive depends on the fashion of the time, physically as well as mentally"—and thus two persons "fall in love" when they feel they have found the best object available on the market, considering the limitations of their own exchange values. The third error, for Fromm, lies in the confusion between the initial experience of "falling" in love, and the permanent state of being in love, or as we might say, of "standing" in love. In other words, the problem of romantic love.

Fromm argues that the "art of loving," like any other art, requires the mastery of both the theory and practice of love. The mastery of the art must be a matter of ultimate concern; here may lie the answer to the question of why people in Western cultures so rarely try to learn this art, in spite of their obvious failures: "In spite of the deep-seated craving for love, almost everything else is considered to be more important than love: success, prestige, money, power—almost all our energy is used for the learning of how to achieve these aims, and almost none to learn the art of loving." Fromm contends that love—"a capacity of the mature, productive character"—is notably absent from contemporary societies. He suggests that no "objective observer of our Western life can doubt that love—brotherly love, motherly love, and erotic love—is a relatively rare phenomenon, and that its place is taken by a number of forms of pseudo-love which are in reality so many forms of the disintegration of love." Automatons cannot love; they can simply exchange their "personality packages" and hope for a fair bargain.[22]

Mother Love

Miguel de Unamuno in *The Tragic Sense of Life* proclaims: "And what is maternal love but compassion for the weak, the stricken, the helpless child in need of milk and a mother's lap? And in women all love is maternal." We will not take issue with the notion that in women "all love is maternal," but rather point to clear differences between maternal or mother love and other forms of love. Once again we are indebted to Fromm's account of the subject; in a vein similar to Bowlby's, he talks of the infant's initial dependence:

> The infant, at the moment of birth, would feel the fear of dying, if a gracious fate did not preserve it from any awareness of the anxiety involved in the separation from the mother and the intra-uterine existence. Even after being born, the infant is hardly different from what it was before birth; it cannot recognise objects, it is not yet aware of itself, and of the world as being outside of itself. It only feels the positive stimulation of warmth and food, and it does not yet differentiate warmth and food from its source: mother. Mother *is* warmth, mother *is* food, mother *is* the euphoric state of satisfaction and security.[23]

Fromm argues that the experience of being loved by mother is a passive one—"*I am loved because I am.* There is nothing I have to do in order to be loved, mother's love is unconditional. All I have to do is *to be*—to be her child." In this account mother's love need not be acquired, it need not be deserved, but there is a negative side, too, to the unconditional quality of mother's love. Not only does it not need to be deserved, it also *cannot* be acquired, produced or controlled. From the child's point of view, if it is there, it is "like a blessing; if it is not there, it is as if all beauty had gone out of life—and there is nothing I can do to create it." But again in a vein quite similar to Bowlby, Fromm argues that other persons become important to the child as he grows and changes.

> The first months and years of the child are those where his closest attachment is to the mother. This attachment begins before the moment of birth, when mother and child are still

one, although they are two. Birth changes the situation in some respects, but not as much as it would appear. The child, while now living outside of the womb is still completely dependent on mother. But daily he becomes more independent: he learns to walk, to talk, to explore the world on his own; the relationship to mother loses some of its vital significance, and instead the relationship to father becomes more and more important.[24]

Fromm points to the differences between motherly and fatherly love. As we have already noted, motherly love is seen as unconditional, but interestingly Fromm adds that unconditional love "corresponds to one of the deepest longings, not only of the child, but of every human being," and therefore "no wonder that we all cling to the longing for motherly love, as children and also as adults." This is precisely the point to which we will return: there is no substitute for mother love. As Fromm puts it, the relationship to the father is quite different: "Mother is the home we come from, she is nature, soil, the ocean; father does not represent any such natural home." Fatherly love is conditional love: "I love you *because* you fulfil my expectations, because you do your duty, because you are like me." The negative side to this is that fatherly love has to be deserved and it can be lost, but on the positive side the child can acquire it—it is not entirely out of the child's control.[25]

Although Fromm's argument might seem a little severe, there is clearly something in it, especially in the later years of a child's life, when the child is growing up. But this should not surprise us. Fathers do not carry the child or give birth and most fathers are not central figures in the child-rearing process, so it is plausible to argue for a difference in the ways that the respective parents love. It is important, however, to stress the fact that the differences between motherly and fatherly love are most prominent in the growing years, a point Fromm makes.

In contrast to brotherly love and erotic love which are love between equals, the relationship of mother and child is by its very nature one of inequality, where one needs all the help, and the other gives it. It is for this altruistic, unselfish character that motherly love has been considered the highest kind of love and the most sacred of all emotional bonds. It seems, however, that the real achievement of motherly love lies not in the mother's love for the small infant, but in her love for the growing child. Actually, the vast majority of mothers are loving mothers as long as the infant is small and still completely dependent on them.[26]

The child, however, must grow, it must become a completely separate human being. The very essence of motherly love, according to Fromm, is to care for the child's growth, and that means "to want the child's separation from herself." Here lies the basic difference between mother love and erotic love. In erotic love, two people who were separate become one. In mother love, two people who were one become separate. The mother must not only tolerate the child's separation, she also must actively encourage it. As Fromm puts it, it is only at this stage that motherly love becomes such a difficult task, that it requires "unselfishness, the ability to give everything and to want nothing but the happiness of the loved one." The conclusion is that it is also at this stage that "many mothers fail in their task of motherly love." Although we all know of mothers who cannot "let go," Fromm's remarks could still be seen as hard or callous, as another way of blaming women, making them scapegoats for history. However, there are two points that we must take with us from Fromm's analysis, both of which are compatible with Bowlby's arguments. First, there can be no such thing as a maternal instinct, because instincts do not disappear; secondly, that mothering is a learned art and skill. This is not to say that no woman knows how to mother and must therefore be told by men how to do so. But mothering is a valuable and onerous task which should never be underestimated.

Fromm is unusual as a psychologist in that he talks about

love, a quality so difficult to conceptualize and certainly impossible to measure; most psychologists have preferred to dismantle love into its constituent pieces (and hence partly to miss the whole point) and describe and study those fragments.

Baby-Mother Relations

Students of psychology spend three years at university studying the subject and rarely discuss human emotions, human sexual relations, mothering (let alone fathering); the mind may only be mentioned in passing. In other words, psychology as it is currently taught in most universities is an odd subject. In many cases it could well be retitled "The Navigational Skills of the Smaller Animal." Ironically, before the Second World War there was considerable interest in developmental psychology, in the relationship between child and mother. In psychoanalysis this has always been a central concern. But as academic psychology has become more concerned with its image—technological and quantitative, as biology and the physical sciences are "supposed" to be—indefinable qualities such as mothering have been largely abandoned. There are, however, a few exceptions.

We have already noted the views of J. B. Watson, who believed the infant to be totally amenable to human shaping— a plastic being—while probably the most famous description of the infant is that of William James who in 1890 talked of the baby who, "assailed by eyes, ears, nose, skin, and entrails all at once, feels it all as one great blooming, buzzing confusion." Nowadays psychologists who study mother-infant relationships seriously focus precisely on the fact that they *are* relationships—two-way processes in which each partner contributes something to the other. Why it has taken so long to reach this conclusion is baffling. Jean-Jacques Rousseau, for example, in

Emile pointed to such a psychological reality as early as the mid-eighteenth century.

> No mother, no child; their duties are reciprocal, and when ill done by the one they will be neglected by the other. The child should love his mother before he knows what he owes her. If the voice of instinct is not strengthened by habit it soon dies, the heart is still-born.

Bowlby himself has always stressed the fact that both partners in the mother-child relationship should "find satisfaction and enjoyment" from their liaison, and has specifically pointed to this fact of reciprocity.

> James Barrie has told us that, when the first baby smiled, the smile broke into a thousand pieces and each became a fairy. I can well believe it. Babies' smiles are powerful things, leaving mothers spellbound and enslaved. Who can doubt that the baby who most readily rewards his mother with a smile is the one who is best loved and best cared for?[27]

Much of the work of the more recent developmental psychologists has focused on the quality of maternal responsiveness rather than the quality of maternal care—an approach partly inspired by Bowlby's work and seen also as a refutation of it. For example, Martin Herbert asserts that the "important thing to remember is that a good mother-child relationship does not depend on being together every minute, day in, day out," rather it depends on what "happens between them when they are together and the quality of care given." He adds that a "loving mother who can enjoy the company of her child after her day's work can have a less fraught relationship with him than a mother who is lonely and resentful about being 'trapped' at home all day or always anxious and unhappy because she cannot make ends meet."[28] There is some truth to this proposition, but we must remember two things. Bowlby placed considerable emphasis on the quality of maternal (or permanent mother substitute) responsiveness. More importantly we must realize that "after her day's work" the average mother will be tired, guilty and also expected to continue with housework; moreover, the infant itself will be tired. But of course some people believe that Bowlby did not emphasize reciprocity. So, for example, we have the comments of Schaffer, who observes that one of the "main achievements of Bowlby's attachment theory" is that it "addressed itself equally to both child and mother, conceiving of them as a unit that has evolved together and in which the two stand in a continuing reciprocal relationship at all stages of the child's development,"[29] while Richard Q. Bell's complaint is that Bowlby "does not speak sufficiently to the social interaction that is the key to socialization."[30]

Much of the early work in developmental psychology which emphasized reciprocity was concerned with such features as "crying" and what it might mean. Silvia Bell and Mary D. Salter Ainsworth, after initial research, concluded that

consistency and promptness of maternal response is associated with decline in frequency and duration of infant crying. By the end of the first year individual differences in crying reflect the history of maternal responsiveness rather than constitutional differences in infant irritability. Close physical contact is the most frequent maternal intervention and the most effective in terminating crying. Nevertheless, maternal effectiveness in terminating crying was found to be less powerful than promptness of response in reducing crying in subsequent months. Evidence suggests that whereas crying is expressive at first, it can later be a mode of communication directed specifically toward the mother. The development of noncrying modes of communication, as well as a decline in crying, is associated with maternal responsiveness to infant signals.[31]

More recently, developmental psychologists have demonstrated unequivocally that babies are not a "great blooming, buzzing confusion" but rather competent newborns. Tom Bower, for example, demonstrated that a "three-day-old infant can learn to turn his head to the left to obtain reward when a bell sounds, and to the right when a buzzer sounds," and moreover "he can learn the bell-left, buzzer-right discrimination in a few minutes." Once he has learnt the response, he can learn very quickly to reverse it if the experimenter switches the signals. Interestingly, there are some skills that only newborn babies possess, and which fade with age. Therefore we should reevaluate the assumption that development is a continuous, step-by-step process, in which older people know all that younger people know.

> Many of the capacities of the newborn fade away in the course of development, some of them never to return. Neonate walking . . . is a case in point. If newborns are held properly, they march along a solid surface in a most impressive manner. This capacity disappears at about the age of eight weeks. The reaching of newborns disappears at about the age of four weeks. Their ability, or perhaps willingness, to imitate goes at about the same time.[32]

Rudolph Schaffer's *Mothering* summarizes serious academic psychology's current view on the mother-infant relationship. Schaffer himself begins with the assertion that "mothering is a highly complex pattern, the more so because it involves two individuals." In other words, due attention must be paid to the peculiarities of both partners. Schaffer summarizes it thus:

> The features of infant behaviour which particularly matter for social interaction are its spontaneity, its periodicity and its selectivity. Since it is spontaneous, the adult is not dealing with an inert, passive organism which he must stimulate into life. The task of the socializing parent is therefore not to create behaviour out of nothing, but rather to synchronize with behaviour which is already organized.[33]

Schaffer sees the mother's relationship with a child as a senior partner, by virtue of being more experienced, more powerful and more likely to have consciously formulated ideas about the purpose of and direction of the interaction. She rarely does anything, according to Schaffer, without being aware of her child's precise requirements or without adapting her behavior in this light, and the younger the child the greater her need to adapt in this way. Schaffer contends that such interpersonal synchrony is particularly evident when we study interactions "microscopically."

> Whether we observe a baby feeding, playing, being bathed, changed and put to bed, or merely being bounced on his mother's knee, we find a highly intricate pattern of interaction—a pattern that is based on the intrinsic organisation of social behaviour but that subsequently develops through the sheer experience of mutual contact.
>
> This takes us a long way from the traditional view of socialisation, which saw this process as a quite straight forward matter of indoctrination: of telling small children about the use of spoons and potties, about the importance of saying thank you and not killing the new baby. The child had to fit into his social group, so one had to shape his behaviour accordingly.
>
> We can now see that one cannot change a child unless one begins with the context of his own behaviour. Change cannot be imposed from the outside; it can only start from within the relationship between parents and child and thus becomes a matter of *mutual* adjustment. The two modify each other continually; they grow with each other. Socialization is a two-way, not a one-way business: like education, it is essentially a *joint* venture.[34]

Schaffer observes that if a mother is asked "what she considers to be the essence of mothering," she will "have no hesitation in replying: love," and he then laments that the subject is not researched in developmental psychology. However, Schaffer, on the basis of evidence that he considers valuable, asserts that "mother need not be the biological mother: *she can be any person of either sex.*" He argues that the ability to rear a child, to love and cherish and care for her, is basically a matter of personality; there is no reason why the mothering role should not be filled as completely by males as by females:

> The human male's relative lack of involvement in child rearing is essentially a cultural rather than a biological phenomenon. Originally, of course, biological factors were involved, in particular the fact that it is the mother who gives birth to the child and that it was she who subsequently had to suckle it for many months to come. Child care of necessity thus used to be woman's business. Add to that the need to use the superior strength of the male to hunt, work the fields and make war, and one finds sufficient reasons for the division of labour almost universal in former times and still prevalent today.[35]

But now, according to Schaffer, three factors suggest that things could be different. First the use of feeding bottles; secondly, the fact that work now demands physical strength only rarely; and, finally, the point that "biologists give us reason to think that even the process of birth, in its natural form, is not sacrosanct—that it may eventually be possible to grow a foetus not in a womb but in an artificial environment from which it is delivered in due course." Thus, he adds, all the "original reasons for confining child care to women are disappearing: *mother need not be a woman.*" Schaffer concludes that in an "ideal child's world, convention would be replaced by personal inclination: whichever parent displayed those qualities that made him [sic] the best match for the child would be in the more favourable position to become primary caretaker."

What does any of this tell us about women's psychology? What do women think of this? Do they want to relinquish the mothering role?

6

Women as Mothers

It is hard to avoid the fact that there is something really depressing about motherhood.
Ann Oakley, *Telling the Truth About Jerusalem*

Pregnancy is barbaric . . . the temporary deformation of the body of the individual for the sake of the species.
Shulamith Firestone, *The Dialectic of Sex*

The child care experts—John Bowlby, Donald Winnicott, and Benjamin Spock—represented not conservative or traditional thinking—which had been far more authoritarian towards children—but a radical new departure in child care, which, they suggested, should be child-centred and permissive. Their views on the upbringing of children, the importance to the child of love, stimulation, and attention were profoundly attractive to a generation of socially progressive mothers in rebellion against the rules, clockwork, and restraint of the Truby King era, when it had been considered wrong to comfort your crying baby or to feed it on demand. . . . Their work was an indictment of élitist upper-class forms of childrearing—nannies and boarding schools—and implicitly working class warmth and spontaneity towards children were validated. Their conservative views on women were acceptable as part of this package.
Elizabeth Wilson, *Only Halfway to Paradise*

MOST mothers do not write books. Most mothers rear their children as if it were a natural duty. Most mothers experience joy and despair in mothering. Not all feminists are mothers. In

135

other words, there is as much sexism in some feminist writing about what women should do with their lives, especially when writing on issues concerning motherhood and child care, as there is in male-dominated advice manuals which also tell women how to run their lives. Bowlby, somewhat naïvely, believes that his own advice is based on "scientific evidence" rather than being a strong, pervasive and immensely plausible *argument,* but at least he is not a professional proselytizer. Much feminist writing on the subject of motherhood has greatly misunderstood Bowlby's work. It is my intention here to look at the most fruitful of the arguments put forward by feminists, the ones that will enable us to synthesize the ideas of Bowlby and the aims of feminism.

There are some factors involved in motherhood and child care to which most women writers, if not all feminists, refer. The first concerns the conditions in which motherhood is carried out by the majority of women. When Ann Oakley talks of the "depressing nature of motherhood" she is talking about the "blues," anxiety, states of depression, dissatisfaction with the role, and ambivalence towards the infant who is being cared for. Like many feminists, Oakley sees that in turning to the "idealized fulfilment of the mother-child relationship" women do not begin to solve their basic problem of an "insufficiently individuated sense of self." Nor do mothers begin to solve this problem for their daughters, and Oakley therefore stresses the importance of the opportunity for nondomestic identification. As she explains:

> There is no doubt that . . . having another work role that is economically rewarding and publicly valued improves the mental health of mothers, probably because it increases their perception of themselves as individuals and adds to (or promises them a basis for) self-esteem. At the same time, children of employed mothers, especially daughters, appear to be more independent, more self-reliant, less "feminine" and less rigid in their conception of gender roles.[1]

Choice is denied to most women: "It has *not* been argued here that all women should be removed from the domestic sphere but it has been argued that women (and men) should be able to choose their major sphere of activity," argues Jacqueline Tivers.[2] Stephanie Dowrick and Sibyl Grundberg concentrate on choices denied to mothers, and assert that motherhood has for so long been the "central fact of women's lives that the idea of *choice,* deceptively linked with such familiar concerns as contraception and the option of abortion, is almost beyond our grasp." They add a familiar complaint: " 'Choice' is meaningless in a society which refuses to accept that responsibility for the care of children should be shared by all who benefit from their existence."[3] And, of course, when mothers do exercise choice and work outside as well as inside the domestic setting, they cannot win. Alison Clarke-Stewart provides an excellent summary of the pros and cons of holding down two occupations at once.

Although husbands of married women who hold full-time jobs are likely to help with the housework and children, there is no equal sharing of tasks between spouses. The primary responsibility and time commitment in most families is still the wife's . . . [and] most mothers holding full-time jobs feel tired and over worked. Many feel lonely and socially isolated, and all feel harried. There are compensations, of course. They get more satisfaction from their work than non-working women do from housework. They feel better about themselves as individuals and as competent achievers. . . . They feel more independent and in control of their own dual role.[4]

But perhaps the most insidious pressure placed upon contemporary women is from those who question the value of children in women's lives in the first place, and from those who, at the other extreme, believe that a woman is not normal if she decides against having them.

The Maternal Instinct?

An increasingly prominent cultural message aimed at women is that if she is socially aware, she rations herself to one or two children, and if she has any sense, she probably decides against having them at all, because only if she does not have children can she really enjoy life and have a good relationship with her mate. As Sheila Kitzinger notes, in this view, the social context of childbearing has become negative and rejecting—"childbearing is an interruption of their 'real' lives." Kitzinger adds that this particular ethos, which downgrades motherhood and child-rearing, attributes to those women who find motherhood satisfying a "mindless, sentimental form of idiocy."[5] Kitzinger believes that in the women's movement—whatever that might be—there is an ambiguous approach to motherhood.

> It represents for some a biological trap associated with the outmoded stereotype of woman as breeder and a method of ensuring her servitude in the home, and for others an opportunity for achieving something which a man manifestly cannot do however hard he tries. There are on the one hand those who actually enjoy birth, breast-feeding and other aspects of biological motherhood, and on the other those who see them as traitors to the whole movement. But whichever position they adopt they are seeking a more realistic view of the family, and are scraping away the varnish of what they believe is a "Sunday supplement dream" held up to women as a model which leaves each one feeling that she cannot cope as well as all the others.[6]

But perhaps the most insidious perspective is that which bases its arguments on the pernicious notion of maternal instinct. Clearly such an instinct does not exist, otherwise all women would want to bear children, and not all women do.

The softer version of the notion—that mothering comes naturally, and is the same all the world round—is equally untrue.

Elizabeth Badinter, in *The Myth of Motherhood*, argues that the maternal instinct is a myth, and that maternal care is a human feeling; like any feeling it is uncertain, fragile and imperfect. She adds that contrary to many assumptions it is not a "deeply rooted given in women's natures"; when we observe the historical changes in maternal behavior, we notice that "interest in and devotion to the child are sometimes in evidence, sometimes not." Bowlby's position, of course, is similar, in that he sees the mother-child relationship as one of *learning*, rather than as a natural expression of given natures. Using historical material from France, Badinter concludes that

> no universal and absolute conduct on the part of the mother has emerged. On the contrary, her feelings, depending on the cultural context, her ambitions, and her frustrations have shown themselves to be extremely variable. How then can one avoid concluding, even if it seems cruel, that mother love is only a feeling and, as such, essentially conditional, contingent on many different factors? The feeling may exist or may not exist; appear and disappear; reveal itself as strong or weak; be focused on one child or lavished on many . . . mother love cannot be taken for granted. When it exists, it is an additional advantage, an extra, something thrown into the bargain struck by the lucky ones among us.[7]

Schaffer, in his book entitled *Mothering*, broadens that geography and in his reflection of the notion he turns to evidence concerning a small tribe on the northern border of Uganda, the Ik. The Ik had formerly been a nomadic tribe of hunters and gatherers, but as a result of government action had been excluded from their most fertile hunting grounds and confined to a limited, barren area in which they were no longer able to support their existence adequately. With starvation came a virtual disintegration of their social organization: the family as an institution almost ceased to exist, and in the wake of the struggle to remain alive there followed an "utterly selfish attitude to life that displaced all positive emotions like love, affection and tenderness."

> Children were regarded as useless appendages who were turned out of the parents' hut when they reached the age of three years, compelled from then on to make their own way without help or guidance from any adult and certainly without any parental love and affection. Consequently one rarely saw a parent with a child except accidentally or incidentally; when a child hurt himself by falling into the fire the only reaction was amusement; if a predator came and carried off a baby the mother was merely glad at no longer having to care for it. One never saw a parent feed a child over the age of three—on the contrary, such children were regarded as competitors from whom food had to be hidden; if consequently one died of starvation that merely meant that one mouth fewer.

Schaffer argues that the Ik are not unique, and points to Margaret Mead's description of the Mundugumor people of New Guinea. Here, too, according to Mead, there is no such thing as mother love, for from birth on a baby finds herself in a society that dislikes children intensely—if, that is, she is allowed to survive, for many babies are simply thrown in the river. As Schaffer notes, such dislike is expressed in every attitude and rearing practice the child encounters: in the quick and peremptory way in which she is suckled, in the sullen resentment with which the mother greets any sickness or accident that may befall her, and in her refusal to let the child "cling to her in fear or affection."[8]

Why? Schaffer conjectures that in the case of the Ik it is due to the need to survive in the face of starvation, while on the other hand the Mundugumor face a situation of abundance. In this state of abundance, however, practically no cooperation is required among individuals and this leaves plenty of scope for violent hostilities to flower in their social life to which the affectionless upbringing of children is, of course, so precisely adapted. Schaffer concludes that "lovelessness has become institutionalised; parents dislike and resent their children, and the inevitability of mother love has therefore to be questioned."[9]

The Mystique of Betty Friedan

As Lynne Segal has recently written, for "many young women in the late 1960s and the early 1970s the women's liberation movement meant liberation from motherhood," but for her, on the other hand, women's liberation meant the "freedom to enjoy motherhood for the first time."[10] For her, motherhood and child care were always a part of feminist thought and action, but, as she observes, there has been a "noticeable shift in feminist writing on motherhood since the late Seventies." Some of these shifts, however, are not as great as many imagine. Take the case of Betty Friedan.

In *The Feminine Mystique,* originally published in 1963, Friedan reported that those studies that show "working women to be happier, better, more mature mothers do not get much publicity." Rather, she suggested, work which undervalued working mothers—studies *similar* to those of Bowlby, for example—was given undue prominence, focusing *not* on the children of educated, middle-class working mothers but on those children who were truly abandoned, virtually at birth. Friedan insisted that there was no firm evidence that children suffered in any material or emotional sense if their mothers worked. As she amusingly put it, parenthood in the 1950s, and especially motherhood, under the "Freudian spotlight," had to become a "full-time job and career if not a religious cult. One false step could mean disaster."

Much has recently been written on the changes in Friedan's thinking, most visible in *The Second Stage,* first published in 1981. It is true that she has altered her opinions somewhat on the priorities for feminist struggle, but she still asserts and amplifies some of her earlier principles, for example on the importance of choice: the "right to choose is crucial to the personhood of woman. The right to choose has to mean not only the right to choose not to bring a child into the world against one's will, but also the right to have a child, joyously, responsibly, without paying a terrible price of isolation from the world and its rewarded occupations, its decisions and actions." Friedan adds that "women can choose motherhood now without paying the price of physical mutilation and short-ening of life that women had to pay generations ago, but that choice is still weighted by the price of psychological mutila-tion, stunting of talents and economic disasters that too many women paid, even in my generation."

Friedan still maintains that the price of motherhood is too high for most women.

> The stunting of abilities and earning power is still a real fear, because professions and careers are still structured in terms of the lives of men whose wives took care of the parenting and other details of life. The point is that *equality*—the rights for which women have been fighting for over a century—was, is, necessary, for women to be able to affirm their own person-hood, and in the fullest sense of choice, motherhood. The point is, the movement to equality and the personhood of women isn't finished until motherhood is a fully free choice.[11]

But in *The Second Stage* Friedan has further thoughts on the subject of motherhood which are extremely instructive. She argues that to deny the part of "one's being as woman that has, through the ages, been expressed in motherhood—nurturing, loving softness, and tiger strength—is to deny part of one's personhood as woman." More particularly Friedan laments the sullenness she observes in "younger women who now are living their personhood as women as if this somehow excludes all those emotions, capabilities, needs that have to do with having babies, mothering children, making a home, loving and being loved, dependence and independence, softness and hardness, strength and weakness, in the family." She is not, of course, suggesting that every woman has to be a mother to "fulfill" herself as a woman, rather she is emphasizing, as she always has, the right to choose. In conclusion, however, she makes further inroads into her original conceptions of the goal of feminism when she observes that it would be a tragic mistake if women were blindly to emulate a narrow male role and thereby fail to understand that the women's movement, and all that it implied, offered women a chance to transcend the rigid barriers of sexual stereotypes and to seek fulfillment in work *and* family.

However, it is to the feminists who have taken motherhood as absolutely central to their analysis that we now turn.

Dorothy Dinnerstein: the Rule of the Cradle

Dorothy Dinnerstein, in *The Mermaid and the Minotaur: Sexual Arrangements and Human Malaise,* produces an argument which, in its description of the *process* of mothering, is at one with Bowlby. Her conclusions, however, are somewhat different.

Dinnerstein argues that women's monopoly of mothering—given that women remained *"almost universally in charge of infant and early child care"*—was the central cause of the human malaise endangering the continuation of life in the late twentieth century. As Hester Eisenstein explains in her brilliant exposition of Dinnerstein's difficult ideas, the core of Dinnerstein's analysis is her contention that the experience of human infancy shaped later consciousness, most acutely in the realm of sexuality, and that presiding over that infancy, for all human beings, was "the presence of a woman."[12] Following the arguments of Melanie Klein, Dinnerstein claims that by definition, the mothering of an infant involved a less than complete satisfaction of a child's wants and needs. It was from this preverbal experience that the infant formed her impressions of profound pleasure and bodily satisfaction in feeding and being washed and changed. And it was from this same experience that the child first felt discomfort, frustration and anger. Inevitably, the mother did not, and could not, satisfy all of the infant's needs immediately, and in some cases she could not or would not satisfy them at all. Thus "the child's first experiences both of intense joy and pleasure and of extreme anger and dissatisfaction" were felt in relation to the person who was initially the child's "entire universe."

From this fundamental fact of the first human relationship, many consequences flowed. To cut a long and very contentious story short, Dinnerstein then states that because of their experience in infancy, men felt an overwhelming need to control women in later life. The autonomy of women, in sexual expression and in other areas of life such as work, was profoundly threatening to men. For this reason, men sought to dominate women in personal relationships, and excluded them from the major areas of life—work and culture—that lay outside of the family. For their part, women acquiesced in these arrangements, because of their own sexual formation. As Eisenstein notes, Dinnerstein's view of patriarchy—"woman's exclusion from history"—stemmed from her analysis of the sexual formation of males and females in childhood, and the creation thereby of a double standard in sexuality. Eisenstein summarizes Dinnerstein's analysis of this process:

> By virtue of being nurtured by a woman, men tended to become polygamous—that is, attached to many women—

while women turned out monogamous—attached to one man—in their preferences. Chiefly this was because, as a result of their memory of the precariousness of maternal availability, men found their need for women so overwhelming, and so threatening, that they had to keep it under control. This they accomplished by separating sex from love, and by thus avoiding a replication of the intense need of one woman experienced in infancy. The need of women, and the feared trauma of repeating the loss of early childhood over and over again, made men institute a fierce control over women and their sexuality, while at the same time refusing to permit, in themselves, the depth of commitment to and involvement with one woman that might endanger them in this primitive way.

Conversely, she argued, the need of their mothers was muted in women, partly by means of the conversion to sexual attachment to the opposite sex, and partly because women carried in themselves a sense of the "maternal richness" that the mother had embodied. Women experienced less anxiety about losing the mother, because they "became" the mother themselves: they were "more self-sufficient than the mother-raised man: what is inside oneself cannot be directly taken away by a rival."[13]

In Dinnerstein's view, men's hatred and fear of women would continue as long as women maintained their monopoly over child-rearing. Women were used as a "scape-goat-idol" for all the ills of human existence.

The only way out is for men to take an equal share in the task of nurturing infants. In this way, Dinnerstein argues, the blame and anger that are now directed exclusively at women would be distributed equally between both genders. The "frustrations and limitations of the human condition would be perceived as an inevitable fact, rather than seeming the fault and responsibility of women." With a change to shared parenting, Dinnerstein predicted a second outcome: the end of male dominance. Male rule in the world stemmed from female rule of the cradle.

The Construction of Gender Identity

Nancy Chodorow, in *The Reproduction of Mothering,* asked how one could account for the fact that women continued to want to mother children, to see themselves as mothers or potential mothers, and to carry out the tasks of mothering, largely to the exclusion of men?

Chodorow's answer was that women came to be mothers, or to want to be mothers, by means of a profound process of psychological character formation. She rejects two widely held views of why women mother—that women are somehow suited by nature and evolution for mothering, and the conventional feminist wisdom that women are forced into mothering by ideology and the pressure of sex-role stereotyping. Mothering was reproduced, Chodorow argues, both at the level of social organization and at the level of individual development by a complex system that depended upon the family for its continuity. As Eisenstein comments, Chodorow pointed to the family as the institution within which the economic and social requirements of society were met by means of the "creation of appropriate personality structures for the roles to be played within it." It was "in the family that children learned to be men and women, and that women learned to be mothers."[14] But for Chodorow, the quality of this learning, for both sexes, was not by means of identification and the learning of a role by imitation, but rather through the development of a psychic structure, the very shape of personality.

The qualities for successful nurturing are embedded in personality—specifically, in the female personality—and could not be learned as an act of the will, or merely through imitation of others. As Chodorow puts it, the nurturing that women do

is not something that can be taught simply by giving girls dolls or telling her that she ought to mother. It is not something that a girl can learn by behavioural imitation, or by deciding that she wants to do what girls can do. Nor can men's power over women explain women's mothering. Whether or not men in particular or society at large—through the media, income distribution, welfare policies and schools—enforce women's mothering, and expect or require a woman to care for her child, they cannot require or force her to provide adequate parenting unless she, *to some degree and on some unconscious or conscious level,* has the capacity and sense of self as maternal to do so.[15]

To explain this, Chodorow turned to those psychoanalytic theorists of "object-relations," who considered that, for an infant to develop normally, it had to move over time through a series of stages. More specifically, from an initial psychological sense of *oneness* and unity with the parent, the infant gradually acquired a realization of the reality of the parent as a separate entity and therefore a sense of its own separateness and integrity. This process, whereby infants acquired the most fundamental sense of self, was in fact "a process that differentiated girls from boys and determined that girls, rather than boys, retained the capacity for parenting."[16] As Chodorow puts it, as infants, girls and boys undergo "different psychological reactions, needs, and experiences, which cut off or curtail possibilities for parenting in boys, and keep them open and extend them in girls."[17]

Chodorow points to the fact that in the "preoedipal period" girls lingered longer in a prolonged and exclusive involvement with the mother, while in boys, this preoedipal attachment was rapidly transformed into an oedipal attachment—a possessive and competitive relationship that included rivalry with the father. A girl's attachment to her mother is exclusive, ambivalent, a continuation of the mother-child relationship in which the boundaries between mother and daughter are not clearly defined. A son, however, identifies his mother as someone clearly different to himself at a much earlier stage.

The source of this difference, argues Chodorow, is the

asymmetry caused by the fact that both girls and boys were usually raised by mothers—specifically, it grew out of the fact that mothers perceived and treated their girl children as continuous with themselves, while they treated their boy children as separate from and other than themselves. From this Chodorow argues that for most women, the primary attachment remained to the mother.

As a result of this prolonged and primary attachment to their mothers, girls develop a particular capacity to form and sustain relationships—what Chodorow calls the "relational potential." Eisenstein defines this potential:

> They retained a greater capacity for empathy with others, and they experienced themselves as less sharply separated from other persons, and from the "object-world" in general. In addition, they retained the capacity to "regress" to a less individuated state, and to experience themselves as connected to others, a capacity crucial to the mothering function. Girls did not experience this sense of relatedness and connection as threatening to their sense of self and identity. In contrast, boys, in whom separateness and difference, rather than sameness and continuity, had been stressed by the mother, experienced themselves as more sharply separate from other people and things, and found regression to pre-Oedipal "relational modes" more threatening to the sense of self.[18]

Importantly for Chodorow's account, in the oedipal period (infantile sexual attraction to the parent of the opposite sex), when girls turned to their fathers as objects of sexual desire, they nonetheless retained a "profound attachment to their mothers" from the preoedipal period. As Eisenstein explains, their experience of sexuality in the "prelatent period" was thus of a "triangular, rather than of a dyadic relationship." Women thus had a more complex psychic structure than men. Their sexual attachments constituted a "triangle of infant–mother–

father," with the primary connection between the daughter
and mother, and the connection to the father remaining sec-
ondary.[19] These differences, Chodorow argues, impel women
to become mothers in later life. Eisenstein explains:

> Their greater capacity for self-in-relationship, and their original
> experience of the Oedipal triangle ensured that women, rather
> than men, reared children. The significance of the triangle was
> that, in later life, women were impelled to recreate their infan-
> tile experience by having an infant of their own. They sought to
> reproduce the Oedipal triangle of infant–mother–father with
> its points realigned as mother–infant–father (although
> Chodorow did not make this explicit). During childhood the
> axis of mother-daughter closeness dominated while the daugh-
> ter-father connection was less intense. In adulthood, this psy-
> chic structure impelled women to recreate the primal triangle.
> The mother-infant dyad recaptured the primary intensity from
> the side of the adult who was once more the child.[20]

Chodorow can only conclude that the creation of gender
differences within the family has fateful consequences for
women—women's mothering is the primary cause of the sexual division of labor, and of the continued dominance of
women by men. Eisenstein compares the approaches of Dinnerstein and Chodorow:

> On the significance of mothering for the perpetuation of male
> dominance, Chodorow differed from Dinnerstein, who
> focused on the unappeased anger of both men and women over
> their infantile experience of capricious female power as a cause
> of their continuing acquiescence in the control of women by
> men. In contrast, Chodorow emphasised the unconscious need
> of women to reproduce their infantile experience when adults.
> In a sense, then, Dinnerstein saw female mothering as a source
> of rage, while Chodorow saw it as a seductive locus of connect-
> edness and intimacy.[21]

Motherhood as "Experience" and "Institution"

Adrienne Rich, in her moving and powerful account of motherhood, *Of Woman Born*, begins by talking of the imprint of an experience we carry for life, even into our dying, namely the experience of being born of woman.

> All human life on the planet is born of woman. The one unifying, incontrovertible experience shared by all women and men is that months-long period we spend unfolding inside a woman's body. Because young humans remain dependent upon nurture for a much longer period than other mammals, and because of the division of labour long established in human groups, where women not only bear and suckle but are assigned almost total responsibility for children, most of us first know love and disappointment, power and tenderness, in the person of a woman. [22]

Rich, who in the above passage could be the author of Bowlby's *Attachment,* distinguishes two meanings of motherhood, "one superimposed on the other": "the *potential relationship* of any woman to her powers of reproduction and to children; and the *institution,* which aims at ensuring that that potential—and all women—shall remain under male control."

Motherhood, according to Rich, involved suffering and deprivation for most women under patriarchy. Throughout history numberless women have "killed children they knew they could not rear, whether economically or emotionally, children forced upon them by rape, ignorance, poverty, marriage, or by the absence of, or sanctions against, birth control and abortion." More personally, Rich asks:

> What woman, in the solitary confinement of a life at home enclosed with young children, or in the struggle to mother them while providing for them single-handedly, or in the conflict of weighing her own personhood against the dogma that

says that she is a mother, first, last, and always—what woman has not dreamed of "going over the edge" of simply letting go, relinquishing what is termed her sanity, so that she can be taken care of for once, or can simply find a way to take care of herself?[23]

Yet under such conditions of patriarchy the experience of motherhood, in Rich's account, could suggest an alternative: it contained within itself the potential for great creativity and joy. It was not, then, the fact of women's capacity to reproduce that was the basis of women's enslavement, but rather the mode by which that fact had become integrated into the system of male political and economic power over women. Once that system had been dismantled, then motherhood itself would become a transformed and *transforming* experience for women. Destroying motherhood as an institution is not to abolish motherhood itself, according to Rich, but to raise the status of motherhood to the equivalent of "any other difficult but freely chosen *work.*"

Rich saw the dismantling of the institution of motherhood and the subsequent "repossession by women of their bodies" as a far more important change than workers seizing the means of production. Women freed from the institution of motherhood would become the creators of a "new relationship to the universe."

> The mother's battle for her child—with sickness, with poverty, with war, with all the forms of exploitation and callousness that cheapen human life—needs to become a common human battle, waged in love and in the passion for survival. But for this to happen, the institution of motherhood must be destroyed.[24]

Cycles of Mothering

What has been described, in quite different ways, in the previous pages is the cycle of motherhood—why women continue to reproduce even when it may well be to their (and their daughters') disadvantage to do so. Nancy Friday, in her much maligned book *My Mother/Myself,* focuses on some of the beneficial consequences of this cycle, and in so doing gives a further explanation as to why it occurs. She argues that with age, the tie to the mother is weakened by physical or psychological separation, while at the same time "introjection gathers momentum." In all important adolescent and adult rites of passage that take us away from mother, in fact "as we take one step forward, we take another one back, and find ourselves doing things her way." *"Becoming like* [our mothers] *overcomes our separation anxieties."* This introjection is a kind of symbolic rapprochement, in that just as the infant who "crawls away from mama into the next room gets frightened and rushes back for confirmation that she is still there, so, emotionally, as we edge away from mother in our adult lives, do we incorporate parts of her." Friday argues that "having her with us—*in* us— makes the journey less fearsome." "When we become mothers ourselves introjection speeds up even more. When we hold our little girl in our arms, we are reminded of mother, feel at one with her, as never before."

Judith Arcana looks at this matter more socioeconomically, concentrating in a more traditional manner on sex-role stereotyping and its function in the reproduction of mothering. In one of her books, *Every Mother's Son,* subtitled *The Role of Mothers in the Making of Men,* she states that "women create men . . . we carry them inside of our bodies, feeding them with our food, sharing our precious oxygen with them. We labor to bring them to birth, then lift them up into our arms, and hold them warm against our breasts. We soothe, kiss, cuddle, and sing to all the baby men." But then, Arcana adds, "before we realize it's done, they are adult men, culturally empowered to dominate us." She asks how this happens. Her answer, again, concerns the *institution* of motherhood created by patriarchy:

> Men, no matter how sympathetic, no matter how willing to do
> child care, no matter how many studies they've read or done on

the subject, have never been mothers. Despite the now fashionable use of the word "parenting," the raising of children has remained *mothering*. The motherhood institution men have created is built upon their memories of dependence, and on the needs, desires, and fantasies that boys and men have developed about women.[25]

In her other major work, *Our Mothers' Daughters,* Arcana discusses the ambivalence towards motherhood that she herself feels, in common with the mothers she studies. She writes that "our bodies haven't lost the ability to lock into old patterns." Although women are alienated from their bodies in other spheres of their lives, maternity is the one place, according to Arcana, where they "are allowed, if only partially, to move through some natural sensual responses."

> When I became pregnant, I was made aware of my body in ways that even the society around me considered positive. Unlike the usual body-consciousness of women, that constant anxiety resulting from objectification and its resultant physical discomfort, the body sensations accompanying a deliberate and healthy pregnancy felt good. I could openly lavish attention on my body, and everyone, including my mother, approved.

In fact, Arcana goes so far as to use the term "maternal instinct" in describing her earlier encounters with her own son: "As we rocked together, I was rapt as I gazed into his face—and he into mine. As the milk flowed, so did 'love.' Now came maternal instinct—triggered by a chemical reaction. Lactation bonded us."[26]

But having said that, Arcana still asks what woman would truly choose the bondage of patriarchal motherhood? Her answer is that a woman is "induced to deliberately bear and raise children to live in this society, to subject herself and her babies to the pain and grief, duplicity and repression required," through the constant flow of sex-role stereotyping, through the rewards of security and praise, balanced against the heavy penalties for women who do not succumb.

Arcana suggests that the "politically conscious" reason for having children in the first place, namely, of wanting daughters, is misplaced: "We seek the revolution in our daughters, forgetting that many of our mothers sought their escape in us, and that we hated them for it, forgetting that our daughters need models and that what we must do is make the revolution in ourselves." Relatedly—and as an addendum to her argument concerning the potency of sex-role stereotyping— Arcana argues that it is important to recognize that the so-called choice to become a mother is also in part the "need/ desire for our own mothers' approval and acceptance." She adds, however, that

> it is shocking and painful, to daughters who hoped maternity would bring the tenderness and comradeship we'd longed for since our childhood, to find that serious and longlasting improvement in the relationship does not automatically ensue; in fact, there are new grounds to quarrel over for those pairs so disposed, and for all of us daughter-mothers, there is the realization that now, we too play a dual role.[27]

Ironic as it may seem, she adds, the majority of women who strive to be different from their mothers find their own motherhood the greatest opportunity to work out the distinction they seek. However, she stresses that whatever the relations between "our mothers and our children, our own mothering, in style and technique, remains based, quite firmly, in the models our mothers have presented." Arcana's argument, however, is more complex than that:

> Even those of us who appear to have gone in the opposite direction—who curb our children's emotional expression because we feel that we suffered from being given "free rein," or who devote time and energy to our children's activities because we felt deprived when our mothers were not scout leaders—we make these compensatory adjustments super-

ficially, without recognition of the fact that motherhood is far more complex than this one-issue vision would suggest. As we are predominantly patterned after our mothers, most of us raise our children by reproducing the emotional dynamic we experienced as our mothers' daughters. . . . Frequently, we reflect our mothers' internalized experience of sex-role stereotyping.[28]

Arcana believes, on the basis of her studies, that women prefer to have female children, or at least children of both sexes, rather than male children, though most women understand that making males will elicit more praise and status. Many women express relief when they fulfill this requirement so that they can "relax, or stop having children altogether." Interestingly, Arcana suggests that perhaps those daughters who do not want to raise male children have understood on some "very deep level that we are creating and nurturing the agents of our own oppression; once we make them, their education as men in this society will pull them from our arms, set them above us, make them the source of our degradation."[29] To prevent that from happening, Arcana urges mothers to enter into conscious struggle with their sons, actively to change the "traditional" definitions of male and female behavior: "Daring to defy the socio-psychological canons that call us emasculating or seductive mothers, we must raise our sons to feel their needs, to truthfully express them. They will be sensitized; they will develop the capacity to nurture, and they will understand that to live thus is to embody and be surrounded by contradictions."[30]

What Do Women Really Want?

Serious feminist writing has made substantial and important progress since the early 1970s. Motherhood and mothering are no longer dismissed as ephemera; they are central and long-

lasting experiences with crucial consequences. More importantly, it is through these experiences and institutions that
history effectively changes. This is not an overstatement. The
struggle for genuine equality for women is not jettisoned in the
focus on motherhood.

Many feminists are now striving to "create the experience of
maternity and family in a non-exploitative way," says Robyn
Rowland,[31] while the feminists Luise Eichenbaum and Susie
Orbach, in their somewhat ambitiously titled *What Do Women
Want?*, argue that

> from our first relationship with our mother, through our friend-
> ships and love affairs, emotional dependency and contact is the
> food that nourishes us. Men and women alike need to have their
> dependency needs met. Knowing that one can rely on others for
> understanding and emotional support allows one to exploit
> one's opportunities in a confident and expressive way.[32]

Maggie Scarf uses the findings of human ethology rather
than psychoanalysis to assert much the same point:

> Perhaps, though, this ancient hunter-gatherer division of sexual
> labors accounts for that greater masculine sensitivity about
> "making it," about gaining control in the wider world, master-
> ing the environment. Does it relate, I wonder, to the fact that
> men seem to get far more seriously depressed about "goal
> failure" issues than they do about problems in emotional rela-
> tionships? And does it correspond, I wonder, to the female's
> apparently greater affiliative needs, her sensitivity to fluctua-
> tions in her love attachments, and her greater input of Self into
> her important relationships?[33]

Perhaps, however, we should finish with a contemporary
American view—in my opinion a somewhat misguided one—
of the mother-child dilemma. Sylvia Ann Hewlett, in *A Lesser
Life: The Myth of Women's Liberation*, sees things all too clearly:

Women need more than equal treatment if they are to find fulfillment in both love and work. They need equal opportunity in education and in the job market—but they also need a plethora of family support-structures that range from job-protected maternity leave to subsidised day care and flexitime. For whether they are in fact mothers or simply have the potential to be mothers, the lives of women are conditioned by and constrained by child-related responsibilities.[34]

7

Why Children?

The greatest regret of my life has always been that I didn't have my baby, Henri's child, in 1925. Nothing in the whole world is worth a baby, I realized as soon as it was too late, and I never stopped blaming myself.

Gloria Swanson, *Swanson on Swanson*

"You really don't believe in political solutions do you?"

"I believe in political solutions to political problems. But man's primary problems aren't political, they're philosophical. Until humans can solve their philosophical problems, they're condemned to solve their political problems over and over and over again. It's a cruel, repetitious bore."

Tom Robbins, *Even Cowgirls Get the Blues*

WHAT of the children? What are *they* anyway, what function do they have in our lives, why do we have them? If Freud is right, and the act of birth is the child's "first experience of anxiety," we certainly owe them something. But to return to our set of questions: what, for example, are children and how should we behave towards them?

Consider the following maxims: "The child's temperament is determined by the day he is born," "Children should be kept inside for the first six months of their lives so they won't get sick," "You should never let a child cry," "You should feed an infant every four hours" and so on. Each of these, at different times in different societies, has been accepted by different people as a directive. As we saw earlier, there has never been a shortage of people telling us—usually through the advice manuals and books—how to behave with infants, and more importantly what kinds of creatures infants really are. Some social historians have gone one step further and suggested that the whole notion of concentrating on a specific age range and terming it "childhood" is misleading and unhelpful.

Do Children Have a History?

The pictures of childhood painted by the vast majority of historians show a surprising degree of similarity. With an "almost monotonous regularity the same idea appears again and again in the discussion of the history of childhood: that there was no concept of childhood in the past," and many authors argue that there was "no appreciation of the needs of children and thus they were neglected—some authors would say systematically ill-treated—by both parents and the state."[1] The majority of historians claim that there has been only a gradual realization that children are different from adults and not merely smaller versions. Accompanying this realization were a growing concern for children, at times a very strict discipline and an increasingly close parent-child relationship. Pollock, however, argues that:

> most researchers in this area would appear to be more con-
> cerned with finding additional evidence to support the argu-
> ment than with critically appraising it. There are a few authors,
> however, who think differently. They believe that both child-
> hood and adolescence were recognised in previous centuries,
> although children may not necessarily have been viewed in the
> same way as children today.[2]

Philippe Ariès's book *Centuries of Childhood,* written in 1960, is the most influential work in the field, and though his sources are taken mainly from French culture and society, they have been seen to apply equally well to the rest of Western society. Of particular importance is his finding that there was no concept of childhood during the Middle Ages. He also suggests that, although there was no awareness of the nature of childhood in previous centuries, this does not mean that children were ill treated. In fact, he argues that, once it was appreciated that children were different from adults, they were subjected to stricter methods of rearing and severer punishments. Pollock summarizes the position of Ariès and similar theorists—for example, Hunt, Shorter, Plumb and de Mause:[3]

> (a) There was no concept of childhood before the 17th century; children were regarded as being at the very bottom of the social scale and therefore unworthy of consideration. . . .
> (b) There was a formal parent-child relationship; parents were distant unapproachable beings and children were something inferior, whose demands and needs were not sufficiently valuable to be met. . . .
> (c) Up to the 18th century, and again in the early 19th century, children were often brutally exploited and "subjected to indignities now hard to believe."

Social historians who have concerned themselves with the subject argue that a concept of childhood appeared from the seventeenth century on, due to a renewal of interest in education; developments within the family; the rise of capitalism; the emergence of some indefinable spirit of benevolence; and the increasing maturity of parents. This concept of childhood developed during the eighteenth and nineteenth centuries until the child was accorded a central role in family life and children's rights were protected by the state.

Lloyd de Mause, for example, is so certain of both the argument and evidence that he interestingly uses it as a "comprehensive theory of historical change"; his "psychogenic theory of history" posits that the central force for change in history is neither technology nor economics, but the "psycho-genic" changes in personality occurring as a result of successive generations of parent-child interactions. For de Mause the history of childhood is a "nightmare" from which we have only recently begun to awaken. The further back in history one goes, he argues, the lower the level of child care, and the more likely children were to be killed, abandoned, beaten, terrorized and sexually abused. De Mause adds, necessarily, that since some people still kill, beat and sexually abuse children, any attempt to "periodize modes of child rearing must first admit that psychogenic evolution proceeds at different rates in different family lines, and that many parents appear to be 'stuck' in earlier historical modes." He also acknowledges class and regional differences, accepting that his "periodization" is therefore a "designation of the modes of parent-child relations which were exhibited by the psychogenically most advanced part of the population in the most advanced countries."[4] The series of modes represent, according to de Mause, a continuous sequence of "closer approaches between parent and child" as generation after generation of parents slowly overcame their anxieties and began to develop the capacity to identify and satisfy the needs of their children. De Mause's modes are well worth quoting in full.[5]

1. *Infanticidal Mode (Antiquity to Fourth Century A.D.)*: . . . When parents routinely resolved their anxieties about taking care of children by killing them, it affected the surviving children profoundly.

2. *Abandonment Mode (Fourth to Thirteenth Century A.D.)*: Once parents began to accept the child as having a soul, the only way they could escape the dangers of their own projections was by abandonment, whether to the wet nurse, to the monastery or nunnery, to foster families, to the homes of other nobles as servants or hostages, or by severe emotional abandonment at home. . . .

3. *Ambivalent Mode (Fourteenth to Seventeenth Centuries)*: Because the child, when it was allowed to enter into the parents' emotional life,

was still a container for dangerous projections, it was their task to mold it into shape. From Dominici to Locke there was no image more popular than that of the physical molding of children, who were seen as soft wax, plaster, or clay to be beaten into shape. . . .

4. *Intrusive Mode (Eighteenth Century)*: A tremendous reduction in projection and the virtual disappearance of reversal was the accomplishment of the great transition for parent-child relations which appeared in the eighteenth century. . . . The child was so much less threatening that true empathy was possible, and pediatrics was born, which along with the general improvement in level of care by parents reduced infant mortality and provided the basis for the demographic transition of the eighteenth century.

5. *Socialization Mode (Nineteenth to Mid-twentieth Centuries)*: . . . The raising of a child became less a process of conquering its will than of training it, guiding it into proper paths, teaching it to conform, socializing it . . . the father for the first time begins to take more than an occasional interest in the child, training it, and sometimes even relieving the mother of child care chores.

6. *Helping Mode (Begins Mid-twentieth Century)*: The helping mode involves the proposition that the child knows better than the parent what it needs at each stage of its life, and fully involves both parents in the child's life as they work to empathize with and fulfill its expanding and particular needs. There is no attempt at all to discipline or form "habits."

Children brought up in the helping mode are "gentle, sincere, never depressed, never imitative or group-oriented, strong willed, and unintimidated by authority." Clearly, either de Mause is overstating his case (or completely wrong), or there are thousands of parents "trapped" in earlier historical modes—or the evidence we see each day is an illusion. However, de Mause's model of historical change is interesting in that he regards the mother-child relationship as central. This is what we have been arguing for here. The trouble with de Mause, however, is that *he* minimizes those other institutions humans create over time—politics, economics, religion, education—which are created by humans, who were once children and reared to become particular kinds of adults, but are nonetheless institutions which independently help shape human behavior and history. And unlike Bowlby there are no biological givens in de Mause's model. Could de Mause (and Ariès et al.) be *wrong* in their history?

Ariès, de Mause and the Problems of "Evidence"

Throughout this book we have been aware of the shortcomings of the "evidence" produced by different protagonists to support their claims, but it is naïve to believe that discussions concerning human affairs are about "evidence." We are, rather, in the area of morality. The history of childhood is another case in point.

Take the use Ariès makes of paintings as evidence that childhood did not exist in the Middle Ages. He argues that there are so few pictures of children because a child was not deemed of sufficient importance to merit a painting. Many pictorial records of the time depict children as miniature adults engaged in adult activities. But as Judith Ennew points out, these were the sons and daughters of the nobility. Painters depicted their *own* children in "charming, domestic portraits which reveal that children were not always viewed as small adults." Even though the "dominant ideology suppressed childhood and used children as pawns in economic and political alliances, a space did exist for the type of childhood which would be recognizable in the twentieth century."[6]

Linda Pollock notes that many historians have subscribed to the mistaken belief that if a past society did not possess the contemporary Western concept of childhood, then that society had no such concept. This, she asserts, is a "totally indefensible viewpoint—why should past societies have regarded children in the same way as Western society today?" Moreover, Pollock adds, "Even if children were regarded differently in the past, this docs not mean they were therefore not regarded as children." Pollock quite candidly argues that

> the sources used to support the received view are suspect and are certainly not a secure enough base to warrant the dramatic generalisations derived from them. The area in fact bears the hallmark of sloppiness: not only are the problems inherent in the sources used rarely considered, but some of the data used and conclusions arrived at are factually inaccurate . . . [for example] Ariès states that children were beaten at school because their *parents* wished them to be, whereas from the evidence contained in the sources used in this study, parents clearly wished no such thing and were prepared to intervene if they considered their child was being punished too severely.[7]

Linda Pollock's own study—*Forgotten Children: Parent-Child Relations from 1500 to 1900,* based on primary sources and autobiographies—comes to quite different conclusions, contradicting Ariès, de Mause et al. completely. Pollock centrally asserts that because most of the authors on the history of childhood were concerned with the severe discipline meted out to children in the past, their accounts of child life have largely been confined to this area. Thus, she argues, the "children of the past are indecipherable figures; little is known about their actual lifestyle." Pollock's study, on the other hand, attempts to bring children and their parents to life and reveal what parents thought of their children, how they attempted to rear them and also how children regarded their parents. Pollock argues that there is much similarity to be found in the depictions of childhood found in her primary sources:

> It is always possible that the adult diarists were presenting an image—it would be very difficult to write an introspective diary without some element of egoism being present—and therefore perhaps did not relate treating their offspring as the

latter actually were treated. A comparison of the child and the adult sample would reveal any such discrepancies. The child diarists, from the evidence contained in their diaries, were not repressed, severely disciplined beings. In fact, they noted less punishment than the adult diarists, which suggests that they were not subjected to a harsh discipline. They seemed to be happy and content with their lives and were clearly attached to their parents. Some of the adolescent diaries describe discord between parents and children, but this rarely continued for long and nearly all of the children kept in close contact with their parents after they had left home.[8]

Pollock considers that there *was* a concept of childhood in the sixteenth century. This may have become more elaborated through the centuries, but, nonetheless, the "16th century writers studied did appreciate that children were different from adults and were also aware of the ways in which children were different—the latter passed through certain recognizable developmental stages; they played; they required discipline, education and protection." For Pollock, the evidence reveals that there have in fact been very few changes in parental care and child life from the sixteenth to the nineteenth centuries in the home, apart from social changes and technological improvements. Nearly all children were "wanted," weaning and teething aroused interest and concern and parents revealed anxiety and distress at the illness or death of a child. Parents, although they may have found their children troublesome at times, seemed to enjoy the company of their children. In Pollock's view, the majority of children were not subjected to brutality, and cruelty to children was not as widespread as has been claimed. Pollock's sources—her diarists—reveal that the parent-child relationship was far from formal, and instances of the closeness of the parent-child bond abound:

> parents who sat up all night nursing their sick offspring; who worried over the latter's education; who were prepared to come to their children's aid when necessary—and the children also

felt free to approach their parents with any problems they might have—who referred to physical contact between themselves and their children and who were also aware of the latter's activities.[9]

In opposition to de Mause et al., Pollock concludes that "evolutionary" theories of childhood are not proven, that there is no dramatic transformation in child-rearing practices in the eighteenth century, and that our method of child care appears to be an enduring one: "Instead of trying to explain the supposed changes in the parent-child relationship, historians would do well to ponder just why parental care is a variable so curiously resistant to change."

Pollock's conclusion can clearly be used as confirmation of Bowlby's ideas, and that is exactly what we shall do, pointing to the implication that it is the deviations from our traditional methods of child care that cause so many problems. How many cases of child (and parental) unhappiness are there, and what can we do about them?

The "Rights" and "Wrongs" of Children

The United Nations' Declaration of the Rights of the Child, dated 20 November 1959, states that "the child shall be protected against all forms of neglect, cruelty, and exploitation." We have failed miserably to protect the child. James Grant of UNICEF, in *The State of the World's Children,* argues that

> by the age of three or four years, 90% of a person's brain cells are already linked and physical development is advanced to the point where the pattern is set for the rest of a person's life. Those early years therefore cry out for protection—both to defend the child's right to life and its right to develop to its full mental and physical potential—and to invest in the develop-

ment of people so that they can more fully contribute to, and benefit from, the well-being of their families and nations.[10]

Grant calls this an "investment in human capital," and summing up the declining investment in today's children (and tomorrow's world) observes that World Bank figures show that the "43 countries with the highest infant mortality rates (over 100 deaths per 1,000 live births) are currently spending three times as much on defence as on health." And he notes that the "worldwide spending on armaments now exceeds the combined incomes of the poorest half of humanity."

Children cannot, of course, fight back. For a start, because of their age, they are denied rights which as adults we consider to be basic human rights. Bob Franklin suggests that children have their freedom and autonomy limited in a number of ways which range from the "relatively unimportant to the highly significant"—in other words, from being put to bed when the parents decide fit, to being denied voting rights. For Franklin, children form a "large, long-suffering and oppressed grouping in society, a silent and unrepresented minority, undeserving of human rights." Apart from being denied political rights, they are economically disadvantaged, legally defined as being passive, considered the property of their parents and finally subjected to parental and educational forms of punishment and discipline.

Franklin asserts, in his somewhat pessimistic and negative account, that there are two major myths concerning childhood. First, there is the myth that the adult treatment of children is based upon respect and a concern to protect the best interests of the child. According to this "idealized perception, children are elevated to a central position in the fulfilled adult life. Children provide the motivation and purpose, as well as much of the meaning, to many areas of adult life." Secondly, he describes what he calls the myth of childhood as a "golden age":

Childhood is a special period of our lives when, because of our innocence and weakness, we are protected from the harshness and adversity of adult life . . . childhood is a period of unconstrained freedom, a time for play, education and learning. . . . It is remarkable that this myth of childhood as a period of freedom, pleasure and discovery can survive when each adult has necessarily lived through this period and experienced at first hand the injustices and frustrations which occur in childhood. The resilience of the myth is even more remarkable in the light of some data about childhood.[11]

He then numbers those children living in poverty—at least a fifth of Britain's childhood population—children in state care, and the incidence of sexual abuse; in the case of Britain, he argues that in 1980 there were 312 cases of incest and 3,109 cases of unlawful intercourse. In 1979, in Britain, there were 8,967 conceptions among girls under the age of sixteen. Citing the National Children's Bureau research, he suggests that between a "quarter and a third of all children and adolescents have had at least one sexual experience with an adult."[12] We have already graphically described the fact of child abuse, but again Franklin attempts to quantify such behavior. For example, in Britain in 1979, the NSPCC had over 50,000 young people listed as being victims of child abuse. He estimates that between 2,400 and 4,600 children are seriously injured each year, 450 physically incapacitated for life; the estimates for child fatalities range from 100 to 750 a year. Franklin adds to these figures the numerous cases of physical abuse—such as corporal punishment—which are readily accepted as part of a system of discipline in educational and welfare institutions. And of these cases, he estimated that in England and Wales, a "child is beaten once every nineteen seconds of the teaching day, culminating in a quarter of a million beatings per annum." He concludes that "during the International Year of the Child [1985] 15 million children died from starvation, with 10.3 million of those deaths occurring in the first eleven months of the child's life . . . 100 million suffered from malnutrition. "

According to Vincent Fontana, the United States Children's Bureau estimates that from 50,000 to 75,000 incidents of child abuse occur each year in that country. Dr. Vincent De Francis of the Children's Division of the American Humane Association estimates that 10,000 children are severely battered every year, at least 50,000 are sexually abused, 100,000 are emotionally neglected, and another 100,000 are physically, morally, and educationally neglected.[13]

Why Do We Have Children?

There are in a sense as many answers to this question as there are parents. However, certain sociological, cultural and psychological patterns emerge.

Most married people in contemporary industrial societies have children. As Joan Busfield and Michael Paddon observe, there is "little evidence that many are choosing to remain childless throughout marriage." In postwar Britain, nine out of ten women who marry have had at least one child. Busfield and Paddon, on asking couples "Why children?," were regularly and predictably told that they "make a marriage" and they "make a family."[14] Modern demographics complicate the issue: in Sweden, 40 percent of children born are conceived outside of marriage; unmarried mothers announce the birth of their children in the newspapers. Adam Kuper observes, in relation to cohabitation, that

> "living together" is not just marriage without the wedding. For one thing, couples living together are remarkably infertile . . . it sometimes seems almost as though the ancient institution of the family is splitting in two. Childbearing has less and less to

do with pairing off in a stable fashion. Young people "living together" make homes without children. More and more middle aged couples live alone, in what sociologists coyly term the "empty nest," their children having grown up and moved out. [15]

There are surely more significant reasons for desiring to have children. Busfield and Paddon speculate that children are not only satisfying because they are interesting to care for and bring up; they are also satisfying because they "ensure a continuity of individual characteristics and give a sense of keeping part of oneself alive. Having a child is one way of ensuring some sort of indirect immortality for oneself."

But for many women, the reasons for motherhood are connected with marriage, or at least a partner, and are powerfully felt. It is a question of love. Sylvia Plath wrote of infertility:

> Everything has gone barren. I am part of the world's ash, something from which nothing can grow, nothing can flower or come to fruit. In the lovely words of 20th century medicine, I can't ovulate. Or don't. Didn't this month, didn't last month. For ten years I may have been having cramps and for nothing. I have worked, bled, knocked my head on walls to break through to where I am now. With the one man in the world right for me, the one man I could love. I would bear children until my change of life if that were possible. I want a house for our children, little animals, flowers, vegetables, fruits. [16]

No one can deny such powerfully expressed feelings: having a child adds something to life. It changes emotions. Women (and men in a different way) are never the same again. Some women have children because everything else is denied them. Ann Oakley wrote that children are the "inalienable property of women, who otherwise are placed by society in a propertyless condition. They symbolize achievement in a world where under-achievement is the rule." Women in poverty bear children because a child gives them something and, when things go well, ensures some kind of contentment. Children bring hope. This is expressed in the following account by a woman from Georgia in the 1960s:

> To me, having baby inside me is the only time I'm really alive. I know I can make something, do something, no matter what color my skin is, and what names people call me. When the baby gets born I see him, and he's full of life, or she is; and I think to myself that it doesn't make any differences what happens later, at least now we've got a chance or the baby does.[17]

Yet such desires do not always work out when translated into realities. Children are abused; children bring pain and suffering in greater quantities than joy; children grow up to hate their parents. Why is this so?

Madonna and Child

As Martin Richards points out, we live in a society that idealizes and romanticizes motherhood and the relationship between parents and child—the Madonna and Child image. In its simplest form, the image is of an ever-loving mother who feels nothing but "contentment and gratification as she devotes all her waking hours to her child."[18] The baby, too, is romanticized as an attractive, ever-smiling person. However, all human relationships contain positive and negative aspects—or as Anna Freud put it, somewhat darkly, "No child is wholly loved"—and that is as true of a relationship between a parent and child as it is of a relationship between two adults. Children arouse anger, frustration and guilt in almost all adults, as well as love and affection. Moreover, children, from birth, are very different from one another. Some are much easier to love than others—a point which attachment theorists are only just beginning to deal with in any detail, although Bowlby's central position on the mother-infant relationship as a two-way process is in no way compromised by the growing realization that temperamental differences in infants are significant and important.

Another consequence of the Madonna and Child imagery is that it produces an "embargo on negative feelings," as Ann Oakley notes. That children "properly" elicit positive not negative feelings is a particular problem for mothers. Oakley argues that this notion of mother-child relations as sacred, in which children can do no wrong, and as the image of a "natural unit," allows "no room for irritation or anger or mere disinterest."[19]

Bowlby has never argued that mothering was either natural or easy—for him the best possible outcome for human society is for the natural mother to take the work of mothering seriously, as work of the greatest importance.

Conclusions

The effect of Bowlbyism on the consciences of many women who had to go out to work—either to provide for their family or to maintain their mental health—goes unrecorded.

Naima Browne, *Untying the Apron Strings*

Attachment and separation anchor the cycle of human life, describing the biology of human reproduction and the psychology of human development. The concepts of attachment and separation that depict the nature and sequence of infant development, appear in adolescence as identity and intimacy; and then in adulthood as love and work.

Carol Gilligan, *In a Different Voice*

AMERICAN and British societies do not appear to believe that the early years are the formative years, and that childhood can make or break us. They are both pragmatic societies, seemingly almost indifferent to the increased incidence of child abuse, neurosis and madness, crimes against the person, states of depression, loneliness and divorce, with the attendant pain and suffering.

On questions of mothering, the political left blindly follows what it considers to be the "correct" feminist line. It fails to see that feminism—putting women's interests first—ranges from concern about play groups and child care to demands for genuine equal opportunities especially in the workplace, to concerns about sexual freedom and lesbianism. It is my contention that both Bowlby and the more modern feminist writers like Rich, Chodorow, Dinnerstein, Arcana et al. offer genuinely useful guidelines.

173

A Question of Work

Sue Sharpe, in her excellent *Double Identity*, in which working mothers speak for themselves, asserts that working mothers are here to stay. Because of market forces—the shift *away* from male-dominated heavy manufacturing industries to female-dominated insurance, banking, advertising, and service industries—and because of psychological factors concerned with identity and self-image, women want to work, argues Sharpe. Some women certainly do. Some women have to, in order to provide for their children and themselves. Some women feel they ought to work, even when their children are very small; they see it as a failure not to do so. And most working mothers, whichever avenue they follow, take guilt home with them as well as work. Viviana Zelizer asks, "Are children in fact becoming emotionally dispensable in the 1980s, both economically and sentimentally useless to ambitious, or financially pressed, work-oriented couples?"[1] It is a conundrum, however, for families are becoming smaller, and women are delaying childbearing, sometimes into their thirties—yet few couples remain childless. But for many of us, the only things of any value in the world are our children. Not because we can dress them up in fancy clothes; not because they can become an extension of us; not because they bestow a certain kind of status on us. Rather, having children offers us the potential to become better people, through the care we provide. In the process, we discover latent emotions, and reach a fuller understanding of our own childhood. More importantly, children represent hope for change. The apparent desire on the part of some women to become exact equals to men in the workplace is based on a strange logic, if we accept that work is often stressful, exhausting, time-consuming, unsatisfying and occasionally even hazardous. An alternative explanation of the fact that many mothers wish to work outside the home is that mothering is undervalued and institutionalized. Radically so. Linda Gordon illuminates the apparent contradiction between the so-called "joys" of motherhood and the tensions and conflicts experienced by many mothers when, in discussing abusers and neglecters of children, she asserts that "child abuse becomes the more interesting and challenging to a feminist because in it we meet women's rage and abuses of power."[2] In other words, women know that what they do as mothers is both meaningful and powerful, yet the conditions in which they carry out their work with children are symbolically, socially, psychologically and materially deprived. There is a vast discrepancy between the ideal of motherhood and its attendant rewards, and the reality, for most women, of in some way failing to achieve that ideal, of remaining frustrated and dissatisfied.

Employment outside the home offers attractive compensations, as an escape from the pressures of motherhood, as a means of fulfillment. Financial circumstances dictate that a good many mothers have no choice but to seek paid work. Whatever the reason, working mothers must deal with the problems of finding an acceptable source of substitute care. To what extent do Bowlby's strictures on the inadequacy of substitute care continue to apply in these circumstances? No one could argue that the combination of working mothers and poor substitute care equals inevitable disaster. Appalling parenting produces effects like recurrent abuse. But the consequences of the earlier equation could well be more insidious. Let me offer a parallel example.

R. D. Laing did a great deal for people who had been classified as mentally ill and who were subsequently ill treated in institutions under the guise of being cured. At the same time, however, he inadvertently "glamorized" psychosis at the expense of neurosis—those little phobias, anxieties and obsessions. Similarly, what I am arguing here is that not all roads from minimal "maternal deprivation" lead to disaster, but that in some cases the effects can be long-lasting, and may take some time to emerge. As Murray Parkes and Weiss, in another context, put it: "Children who, for whatever reason, have not known the consistent presence of a caring and secure parent may be at some special risk of feeling inadequate and insecure as adults in all their close relationships."[3]

The Solution Is Mothering

None of the evil, exploitation and unhappiness so evident in our industrialized (capitalist) societies will disappear unless future generations undergo a radical change in attitude. We should reexamine the institutions that reinforce and perpetuate a society based on the selfish interest of the individual as opposed to the welfare of the wider community: the structures of inequality must be dismantled.

In a way mothering is about individualism—the act of keeping the infant separate from her care-giver depends on it and produces it. But there is in this an irony, as Robert Lane, in his stimulating essay "Waiting for Lefty; the Capitalist Genesis of Socialist Man," suggests:

> Of all the qualities which seemed most central to the prosperity of the socialist cause, something close to individualism is the most important: the individual's belief that outcomes are contingent upon his own acts, his autonomy from collective pressure and authoritative command, his capacity for independent moral reasoning, his belief in himself and his own powers. Only such "individualised individuals," generated by complex and nurturant institutions, can work a collectivist system.[4]

The only way we can create the "good and just" society is through new people. Those new people can only come from women—as Adrienne Rich has so eloquently put it, we are all "of woman born." But in order to make motherhood work in a politically creative way it has to be freed from its institutionalized and repressive shackles. It has to be seen quite simply as the most important piece of work anyone can do. At any level, this may well require economic intervention, transforming motherhood into highly paid work. But such a policy should neither debase the experience of mothering nor disguise the fact that mothers, women, have to create new men as well as women. Mothers somehow have to pass on to their sons those psychological qualities which Chodorow describes—"relational potential"—and which only women currently possess. Their particular sensitivities and abilities, for example, to form and sustain relationships of a nonsexual nature in adult life, which are not based on power. The irresistible inference in the work of the feminists we have discussed is that only women can mother.

None of the above is intended as another subtle attempt to get women back into the kitchen. That is far too crude. No one is arguing that women be denied choice. But those women who decide to be mothers should be economically and psychologically assisted to do so. Institutional arrangements should safeguard their career potential. As Adrienne Rich, for one, has said, only mothers can save us from further unhappiness and the squalid exploitation that we see around us. Men are incapable of doing it. It is not possible for men to experience motherhood. Probably only in future generations—if mothering is held in high-esteem and practiced creatively—will men begin to acquire, from their mothers, some of the psychological qualities needed to form mature relationships with others. Giving children—especially boys—a nonsexist upbringing is not confined merely to supplying a series of acceptable role models. If we accept that sexism and traditional self-interest should be dispensed with, we can begin by instilling greater psychological sensitivity in our children.

If nothing else, John Bowlby has always valued mothers. He has constantly urged us to realize their importance. He has always stressed those economic factors that make the institution of mothering so difficult to undertake. He has always seen relationships (attachments) throughout life as being the meaning of our existence. And he has always argued that if we ignore or tamper with or complicate the mother-child relationship, we do so at our own peril.

Notes

Preface

1. Vincent J. Fontana, *Somewhere a Child Is Crying* (New York: Mentor, 1973), 15.

2. Ibid., 14–15.

Chapter 1 "Expert" Advice

1. Germaine Greer, *Sex and Destiny* (New York: Harper & Row, 1985), 4.

2. Nancy Pottishman Weiss, "Mother, the Invention of Necessity: Dr. Benjamin Spock's Baby and Child Care," in *Growing Up in America,* ed. N. Ray Hiner and Joseph M. Hawes (Urbana: University of Illinois Press, 1985), 303.

3. Benjamin Spock, *Baby and Child Care* (New York: E. P. Dutton, 1945), 445.

4. Ibid.

5. As quoted in Christina Hardyment, *Dream Babies* (Oxford: Oxford University Press, 1984), 13.

6. Ibid., 177.

7. Ibid., 177–178.

8. Hardyment, *Dream Babies,* 178.

9. J. B. Watson, "Experimental Studies on the Growth of Emotions," in *Psychologists of 1925,* ed. C. Murchison (Worcester, Mass.: Clark University Press, 1926), 27.

10. J. B. Watson, *Psychological Care of the Infant and Child* (Salem, N.H.: Ayer, 1928), 140.

11. Cathy Urwin, "Constructing Motherhood: The Persuasion of Normal Development," in *Language, Gender and Childhood,* ed. Carolyn Steed-

179

man, Cathy Urwin, and Valerie Walkerdine (New York: Methuen, 1985), 165.

12. Hugh Jolly, *Book of Child Care: The Complete Guide for Today's Parents* (London: Allen and Unwin, 1981).

13. Ann Oakley, "Normal Motherhood: An Exercise in Self Control," in *Controlling Women,* ed. Bridget Hutter and Gillian Williams (New York: Methuen, 1981), 101.

14. Ibid.

15. Marshall H. Klaus and John H. Kennell, "Maternal-Infant Bonding," in *Maternal-Infant Bonding,* ed. Marshall H. Klaus and John H. Kennell (St. Louis: C. V. Mosby, 1976), 9.

16. Ibid., 11.

17. Ibid., 12.

18. Judith Trowell, "Effects of Obstetric Management on the Mother-Child Relationship," in *The Place of Attachment in Human Behavior,* ed. Colin Murray Parkes and Joan Stevenson-Hinde (New York: Basic Books, 1982), 90.

19. Wladyslaw Sluckin, Martin Herbert, and Alice Sluckin, *Maternal Bonding* (New York: Basil Blackwell, 1984), 18.

20. P. Leiderman, "Human Mother-Infant Social Bonding: Is There a Sensitive Period?" in *Behavioral Development,* ed. K. Immelmann et al. (New York: Cambridge University Press, 1981), 22.

21. Sheila Kitzinger, "Women's Experiences of Birth at Home," in *The Place of Birth,* ed. Sheila Kitzinger and John A. Davis (New York: Oxford University Press, 1978), 141.

22. Jean Liedloff, *The Continuum Concept* (Reading, Mass.: Addison-Wesley, 1975), 81.

23. Ibid., 150.

Chapter 2   John Bowlby and Mothering

1. Susan P. Penfold and Gillian A. Walker, *Women and the Psychiatric Paradox* (Montreal: Eden Press, 1983), 139.

2. John Bowlby, *Forty-four Juvenile Thieves: Their Characters and Home-life* (London: Ballière, Tindall & Cox, 1946), 25.

3. Ibid., 37.

4. John Bowlby, "Why Delinquency? The Case for Operational Research," Report of a Conference on the Scientific Study of Juvenile Delinquency (London: 1949), 35.

5. John Bowlby and James Robertson, "Responses of Young Children to Separation from Their Mothers," *Courrier of the International Children's Center,* Paris, vol. 2 (2) (1962), 131.

6. John Bowlby, James Robertson, and Dina Rosenbluth, "A Two-Year-Old Goes to Hospital," *The Psychoanalytic Study of the Child,* vol. 7 (1952), 82–94.

7. Bowlby and Robertson, "Responses of Young Children to Separation from Their Mothers," 133.

8. Ibid., 13.

9. John Bowlby, *Maternal Care and Mental Health* (Albany: World Health Organization, 1952), 11.

10. Ibid., 12.

11. Ibid., 13.

12. Ibid., 15.

13. R. A. Spitz and K. M. Wolf, "Anaclitic Depression: An Inquiry into the Genesis of Psychiatric Conditions in Early Childhood," *The Psychoanalytic Study of the Child,* vol. 2 (1946), 113–17.

14. W. Goldfarb, "Psychological Privation in Infancy and Subsequent Adjustment," *American Journal of Orthopsychiatry,* vol. 15 (1945), 247–55.

15. Bowlby, *Maternal Care and Mental Health,* 39.

16. Ibid., 59.

17. Ibid., 67.

18. Ibid.

19. Ibid., 67–68.

20. Ibid., 68.

21. Ibid., 69.

22. Ibid., 73.

23. Ibid., 75.

24. Ibid., 90.

25. Ibid., 108.

26. Ibid., 158.

27. John Bowlby, *The Roots of Parenthood* (London: National Children's Home, 1953), 15.

28. John Bowlby, *Can I Leave My Baby?* (London: National Association for Mental Health, 1958), 6.

29. Ibid., 7.

30. Ibid., 3.

31. John Bowlby, "Perspective: A Contribution by John Bowlby," *Bulletin of the Royal College of Psychiatrists,* vol. 5 (1) (1981), 1.

32. John Bowlby, *Attachment and Loss,* vol. 1, *Attachment* (New York: Basic Books, 1983), 222–23.

33. Ibid., 322.

34. Ibid., 340.

35. Ibid., 208.

36. John Bowlby, *Attachment and Loss,* vol. 2, *Separation* (New York: Basic Books, 1973), 237.

37. Inge Bretherton, "Attachment Theory: Retrospect and Prospect," in *Growing Points of Attachment Theory and Research,* ed. Inge Bretherton and Everett Waters, Monographs of the Society for Research in Child Development, vol. 50 (1–2) (1986), 11.

38. John Bowlby, *Attachment and Loss,* vol. 1, *Attachment,* 378.

39. John Bowlby, *Attachment and Loss,* vol. 2, *Separation,* 42.

40. Ibid., 78.

41. H. F. Harlow, "The Nature of Love," *American Psychologist,* vol. 13 (1958), 673–85; and H. F. Harlow and M. K. Harlow, "Social Deprivation in Monkeys," *Scientific American,* vol. 207 (5) (1962), 136.

42. Muriel Beadle, *A Child's Mind* (London: Methuen, 1972), 50.

43. John Bowlby, *Attachment and Loss,* vol. 3, *Loss* (New York: Basic Books, 1982), 39.

44. Ibid., 10.

45. John Bowlby, *Attachment and Loss,* vol. 2, *Separation,* 367.

46. John Bowlby, *Attachment and Loss,* vol. 3, *Loss,* 442.

47. Ibid., 40.

48. Ibid., 41.

49. Charles Rycroft, *Psychoanalysis and Beyond* (Chicago: University of Chicago Press, 1986), 150–51.

Chapter 3   How Right and Wrong Can You Be?

1. David Ingleby, "Development in Social Context," in *Children of Social Worlds,* ed. M. P. M. Richards and Paul Light (Oxford: Polity Press, 1986), 314.

2. Ibid.

3. Jack Tizard, "Psychology and Social Policy," *Bulletin of the British Psychological Society,* vol. 29 (1976), 233.

4. Margaret Mead, *Coming of Age in Samoa* (Magnolia, Mass.: Peter Smith, 1928), 111–13.

5. Derek Freeman, *Margaret Mead and Samoa* (Cambridge: Harvard University Press, 1983), 202.

6. Ibid., 203.

7. D. W. Winnicott, *Home Is Where We Start From* (New York: Norton, 1986), 124.

8. D. W. Winnicott, *The Child, the Family, and the Outside World* (Harmondsworth: Penguin, 1964), 17.

9. Erik Erikson, *Childhood and Society* (New York: Norton, 1964), 223–24.

10. Robin Fox, *Encounter with Anthropology* (San Diego: Harcourt Brace Jovanovich, 1968), 90.

11. J. F. Bernal and M. P. M. Richards, "What Can the Zoologists Tell Us about Human Development?" in *Ethology and Development,* ed. S. A. Barnett (Philadelphia: Lippincott, 1973), 92.

12. N. Blurton Jones, "Comparative Aspects of Mother-Child Contact," in *Ethological Studies of Child Behavior,* ed. N. Blurton Jones (New York: Cambridge University Press, 1974), 321.

13. M. P. M. Richards, "Early Separation," in *Child Alive,* ed. Roger Lewin (London: Temple Smith, 1975), 23.

14. Barbara Tizard, "The Care of Young Children," *Thomas Coram Research Unit Working and Occasional Papers* (London: University of London Institute of Education, 1986), 2.

15. Ann M. Clarke and A. D. B. Clarke, *Early Experience: Myth and Evidence* (London: Open Books, 1976), 268.

16. Anna Freud and Sophie Dann, "An Experiment in Group Upbringing," *The Psychoanalytic Study of the Child,* vol. 6 (1951), 127.

17. Michael Rutter, *Maternal Deprivation Reassessed* (Harmondsworth: Penguin, 1972), 107.

18. Sarah Moskovitz, "Longitudinal Follow-Up of Child Survivors of the Holocaust," *Journal of the American Academy of Child Psychiatry,* 24 (4) (1985), 407.

19. T. G. R. Bower, *A Primer of Infant Development* (San Francisco: W. H. Freeman, 1977), 157.

20. Rutter, *Maternal Deprivation Reassessed,* 217.

21. Helen Graham, "Maternal Deprivation," in *Children Growing Up,* ed. Alan Branthwaite and Don Rogers (New York: Taylor & Francis, 1985), 19.

22. Denise Riley, *War in the Nursery* (Topsfield, Mass.: Salem House, 1984), 116.

23. Naima Browne, "Do the Gentlemen in Whitehall Know Best? An Historical Perspective of Pre-School Provision in Britain," in *Untying the Apron Strings,* ed. Naima Browne and Pauline France (Milton Keynes: Open University Press, 1986), 20.

24. *Hansard,* June 12, 1947.

25. Carl Corter, "Infant Attachments," in *New Perspectives in Child Development,* ed. B. Foss (Harmondsworth: Penguin, 1974), 179.

26. Jerome Bruner, *The Relevance of Education* (New York: Norton, 1971), 178.

27. F. V. Smith, *Attachment of the Young* (Edinburgh: Oliver and Boyd, 1969), 99–100.

28. Andrea Pound, "Attachment and Maternal Depression," in *The Place of Attachment in Human Behavior,* ed. Colin Murray Parkes and Joan Stevenson-Hinde (New York: Basic Books, 1982), 121.

29. John Bowlby, *Maternal Care and Mental Health* (Albany: World Health Organization, 1952), 11.

30. Andrea Pound, "Attachment and Maternal Depression," 129.

31. H. R. Schaffer, *Mothering* (Cambridge: Harvard University Press, 1977), 92.

32. Vincent J. Fontana, *Somewhere a Child Is Crying* (New York: Mentor, 1973), 99–100.

33. John Bowlby, Karl Figlio, and Robert M. Young, "An Interview with John Bowlby on the Origins and Reception of His Work," *Free Associations,* vol. 6 (1986), 43.

34. David Aberbach, "Loss and Dreams," *International Review of Psycho-Analysis* 11 (1984), 383.

35. Ibid., 393.

36. Ibid.

Chapter 4 Will Daddy (or Day Care) Do?

1. Elyce Wakerman, *Father Loss* (New York: Doubleday, 1984), 55, 114.

2. Ibid., 222.

3. Charles Lewis, *Becoming a Father* (New York: Taylor & Francis, 1986), 1.

4. Christina Hardyment, *Dream Babies* (Oxford: Oxford University Press, 1984), 288.

5. John Newson and Elizabeth Newson, *Patterns of Infant Care* (Harmondsworth: Penguin, 1965), 147.

6. Lewis, *Becoming a Father,* 129.

7. Ann Oakley, *The Sociology of Housework* (New York: Pantheon, 1975), 179.

8. Judy Dunn and Carol Kendrick, *Siblings* (Cambridge: Harvard University Press, 1982), 210.

9. Judy Dunn, *Sisters and Brothers* (Cambridge: Harvard University Press, 1985), 92.

10. Brigid McConville, *Sisters: Love and Conflict within the Lifelong Bond* (London: Pan, 1985), 187.

11. Zick Rubin, *Children's Friendship* (Cambridge: Harvard University Press, 1980), 21.

12. Jonathan Gathorne-Hardy, *The Rise and Fall of the British Nanny* (London: Hodder & Stoughton, 1972), 309.

13. Alison Clarke-Stewart, *Day Care* (Cambridge: Harvard University Press, 1982), 17.

14. Ibid., 13–14.

15. Ibid., 19–25.

16. See, for example, Daniel Yankelovich, *New Rules: Searching for Self-Fulfillment in a World Turned Upside Down* (New York: Random House, 1981).

17. Clarke-Stewart, *Day Care,* 70.

18. Martin Herbert, *Caring for Your Children* (New York: Basil Blackwell, 1985), 52.

19. Jerome Bruner, *Under Five in Britain* (London: Grant McIntyre, 1980), 198.

20. Clarke-Stewart, *Day Care,* 42.

21. Bruner, *Under Five in Britain,* 179.

22. Ibid.

23. Bruno Bettelheim, *The Children of the Dream* (New York: Avon, 1970), 335.

24. Gathorne-Hardy, *The Rise and Fall of the British Nanny,* 328.

25. Mike Stein and Kate Carey, *Leaving Care* (New York: Basil Blackwell, 1986), 34–35.

26. Jack Tizard and Barbara Tizard, "The Institution as an Environment for Development," in *The Integration of a Child into a Social World,* ed. M. P. M. Richards (New York: Cambridge University Press, 1974), 150.

27. June Thoburn, Anne Murdoch, and Alison O'Brien, *Permanence in Child Care* (New York: Basil Blackwell, 1987), 191.

28. Polly Toynbee, *Lost Children: The Story of Adopted Children Searching for Their Mothers* (London: Coronet, 1987), 128.

29. Ibid., 223.

Chapter 5   What Happens When Things Go Wrong?

1. Benjamin Spock, *Baby and Child Care* (New York: E. P. Dutton, 1945), 443.

2. Ann Mitchell, *Children in the Middle* (New York: Methuen, 1985), 190.

3. Ibid., 191.

4. Jacqueline Burgoyne, Roger Ormrod, and Martin Richards, *Divorce Matters* (Harmondsworth: Penguin, 1987), 124.

5. Ibid., 126.

6. Judith S. Wallerstein and Joan B. Kelly, *Surviving the Breakup* (New York: Basic Books, 1982), 59.

7. Jacqueline Burgoyne, Roger Omrod, and Martin Richards, *Divorce Matters*, 128, 130.

8. R. D. Laing, *The Politics of Experience* (Harmondsworth: Penguin, 1967), 13.

9. Michele Barrett and Mary McIntosh, *The Anti-Social Family* (London: Verso, 1982), 51.

10. Ann Oakley, *Telling the Truth About Jerusalem* (New York: Basil Blackwell, 1986), 63.

11. Jon Bernardes, "In Search of the 'Family'—Analysis of the 1981 United Kingdom Census: A Research Note," *Sociological Review,* vol. 27 (1986), 833.

12. Vance Packard, *A Nation of Strangers* (London: McKay, 1972), 49.

13. Michael Young and Peter Willmott, *Family and Kinship in East London* (New York: Penguin, 1963), 60.

14. Peter Laslett, *Family Life and Illicit Love in Earlier Generations* (New York: Cambridge University Press, 1977), 166.

15. Adam Kuper, "Plus ça Change," *New Society* (March 20, 1987), 30.

16. Christopher Iasch, *The Minimal Self* (New York: Norton, 1984), 186.

17. Ibid., 187.

18. Ibid., 190.

19. Jacqueline Burgoyne, "Material Happiness," *New Society* (April 10, 1987), 13.

20. M. de Courcy Hinds, "They Fell in Love at First Sight," *New York Times* (February 14, 1981), 13.

21. Maurice Lamm, *The Jewish Way in Love and Marriage* (San Francisco: Harper & Row, 1980), 12.

22. Erich Fromm, *The Art of Loving* (New York: Harper & Row, 1956), 12.

23. Ibid., 37.

24. Ibid., 39–40.

25. Ibid., 40.

26. Ibid., 46.

27. John Bowlby, *Can I Leave My Baby?* (London: National Association for Mental Health, 1958), 8.

28. Martin Herbert, *Caring for Your Children* (New York: Basil Blackwell, 1985), 52.

29. H. Rudolph Schaffer, *The Child's Entry into a Social World* (San Diego: Academic Press, 1984), 4.

30. Richard Q. Bell, "Contributions of Human Infants to Care-giving and Social Interaction," in *The Effect of the Infant on Its Caregiver*, ed. Michael Lewis and Leonard A. Rosenblum (New York: John Wiley, 1974), 9.

31. Silvia M. Bell and Mary D. Salter Ainsworth, "Infant Crying and Maternal Responsiveness," *Child Development* 43 (1972), 1171.

32. T. G. R. Bower, "Competent Newborns," in *Child Alive*, ed. Roger Lewin (London: Temple Smith, 1975), 123.

33. Rudolph Schaffer, *Mothering* (Cambridge: Harvard University Press, 1977), 44.

34. Ibid., 84.

35. Ibid., 112.

Chapter 6 Women as Mothers

1. Ann Oakley, *Telling the Truth About Jerusalem* (New York: Basil Blackwell, 1986), 64.

2. Jacqueline Tivers, *Women Attached* (Wellesley, Mass.: St. Martin, 1985), 271.

3. Stephanie Dowrick and Sibyl Grundberg, "Introduction," in *Why Children?*, ed. Dowrick and Grundberg (San Diego: Harcourt Brace Jovanovich, 1981), 7.

4. Alison M. Clarke-Stewart, *Day Care* (Cambridge: Harvard University Press, 1982), 12.

5. Sheila Kitzinger, *Women As Mothers* (New York: Random House, 1979), 30.

6. Ibid., 47.

7. Elizabeth Badinter, *The Myth of Motherhood* (London: Souvenir Press, 1981), 327.

8. Rudolph Schaffer, *Mothering* (Cambridge: Harvard University Press, 1977), 90.

9. Ibid., 91.

10. Lynne Segal, "Women's Retreat into Motherhood," *New Statesman* (January 1, 1987), 16.

11. Betty Friedan, *The Second Stage* (New York: Summit Books, 1981), 87.

12. Hester Eisenstein, *Contemporary Feminist Thought* (Boston: G. K. Hall, 1984), 80–81.

13. Ibid., 82–83.

14. Ibid., 88.

15. Nancy Chodorow, *The Reproduction of Mothering* (Berkeley: University of California Press, 1978), 33.

16. Eisenstein, *Contemporary Feminist Thought*, 90.

17. Chodorow, *The Reproduction of Mothering*, 91.

18. Eisenstein, *Contemporary Feminist Thought*, 92.

19. Ibid., 93.

20. Ibid.

21. Ibid., 95.

22. Adrienne Rich, *Of Woman Born* (New York: Norton, 1976), 11.

23. Ibid., 279.

24. Ibid., 280.

25. Judith Arcana, *Every Mother's Son* (Seattle: The Seal Press Feminist, 1986), 97.

26. Judith Arcana, *Our Mothers' Daughters* (Berkeley: Shameless Hussy, 1979), 175.

27. Ibid., 186.

28. Ibid., 193.

29. Ibid., 199.

30. Ibid.

31. Robyn Rowland, "Reproductive Technologies: The Final Solution to the Women Question?" in *Test-Tube Women,* ed. Rita Arditti, Renate Duelli Klein, and Shelley Minden (New York: Methuen, 1984), 358.

32. Luise Eichenbaum and Susie Orbach, *What Do Women Want?* (New York: Putnam Publishing Group, 1983), 174.

33. Maggie Scarf, *Unfinished Business* (New York: Doubleday, 1980), 86.

34. Sylvia Ann Hewlett, *A Lesser Life: The Myth of Women's Liberation* (New York: Warner, 1987), 267.

Chapter 7   Why Children?

1. Linda A. Pollock, *Forgotten Children: Parent-Child Relations from 1500– 1900* (New York: Cambridge University Press, 1984), 1.

2. Ibid.

3. Ibid., 262.

4. Lloyd de Mause, "The Evolution of Childhood," in *The History of Childhood,* ed. Lloyd de Mause (New York: Psychohistory Press, 1974), 51.

5. Ibid., 51–53.

6. Judith Ennew, *The Sexual Exploitation of Children* (New York: St. Martin's Press, 1986), 13.

7. Pollock, *Forgotten Children,* 263.

8. Ibid., 264.

9. Ibid., 268.

10. UNICEF Staff and James P. Grant, eds. *The State of the World's Children* (New York: Oxford University Press, 1983), 72.

11. Bob Franklin, "Introduction," in *The Rights of Children,* ed. Bob Franklin (New York: Basil Blackwell, 1986), 4.

12. Ibid., 5.

13. Vincent J. Fontana, *Somewhere a Child Is Crying* (New York: Mentor, 1973), 35.

14. Joan Busfield and Michael Paddon, *Thinking About Children* (New York: Cambridge University Press, 1977), 133.

15. Adam Kuper, "Plus ça Change," *New Society* (March 20, 1987), 29.

16. Sylvia Plath, *The Journals of Sylvia Plath* (New York: Doubleday, 1982), 29.

17. As quoted in Nancy Caldwell Sorel, *Ever Since Eve* (New York: Oxford University Press, 1984), 28.

18. M. P. M. Richards, "Non-Accidental Injury to Children in an Ecological Perspective," DHSS Conference Paper (June 1974), 2.

19. Ann Oakley, *Subject Women* (New York: Pantheon, 1981), 223.

Conclusions

1. Viviana A. Zelizer, *Pricing the Priceless Child* (New York: Basic Books, 1985), 222.

2. Linda Gordon, "Feminism and Social Control: The Case of Child Abuse and Neglect," in *What Is Feminism?,* ed. Juliet Mitchell and Ann Oakley (New York: Pantheon, 1986), 69.

3. Colin Murray Parkes and Robert S. Weiss, *Recovery from Bereavement* (New York: Basic Books, 1983), 124.

4. Robert E. Lane, "Waiting for Lefty: The Capitalist Genesis of Socialist Man," *Theory and Society,* vol. 6 (1978), 24.

Bibliography

Aberbach, David. "Loss and Dreams." *International Review of Psycho-Analysis* 11 (1984): 383–98.

Ainsworth, M. D. S. *Infancy in Uganda: Infant Care and the Growth of Attachment.* Baltimore: The Johns Hopkins Press, 1967.

Arcana, Judith. *Every Mother's Son.* Seattle: The Seal Press, 1986.————. *Our Mothers' Daughters.* Berkeley: Shameless Hussy, 1979.

Archer, John, and Barbara Lloyd. *Sex and Gender.* New York: Cambridge University Press, 1985.

Arditti, Rita, Renate Duelli Klein, and Shelley Minden, eds. *Test-Tube Women.* New York: Methuen, 1984.

Ariès, Philippe. *Centuries of Childhood.* New York: Random House, 1965.

Badinter, Elizabeth. *The Myth of Motherhood.* London: Souvenir Press, 1981.

Barnett, S. A., ed. *Ethology and Development.* Philadelphia: Lippincott, 1973.

Barrett, Michele, and Mary McIntosh. *The Anti-Social Family.* London: Verso, 1982.

Beadle, Muriel. *A Child's Mind.* London: Methuen, 1972.

Bell, Richard Q. "Contributions of Human Infants to Caregiving and Social Interaction." In *The Effect of the Infant on Its Caregiver.* See Lewis and Rosenblum, eds., 1974: 1–19.

Bell, Silvia M., and Mary D. Salter Ainsworth. "Infant Crying and Maternal Responsiveness." *Child Development* 43 (1972): 1171–90.

Bernal, J. F., and M. P. M. Richards. "What Can the Zoologists Tell Us About Human Development?" In *Ethology and Development.* See Barnett, ed., 1973: 88–103.

Bernardes, Jon. "In Search of 'The Family'—Analysis of the 1981 United Kingdom Census: A Research Note." *Sociological Review* 27 (1986): 826–36.

Bettelheim, Bruno. *The Children of the Dream*. New York: Avon, 1970.

Blurton Jones, N. "Characteristics of Ethological Studies of Human Behavior." In *Ethological Studies of Child Behavior*. See Blurton Jones, ed., 1972: 3–33.

————. "Comparative Aspects of Mother-Child Contact." In *Ethological Studies of Child Behavior*. See Blurton Jones, ed., 1972: 305–28.

————. "Ethology and Early Socialization." In *The Integration of a Child into a Social World*. See Richards, ed., 1974: 263–93.

————, ed. *Ethological Studies of Child Behavior*. New York: Cambridge University Press, 1974.

Boulton, Mary Georgina. *On Being A Mother*. New York: Methuen, 1984.

Bower, T. G. R. "Competent Newborns." In *Child Alive*. See Lewin, ed., 1975: 112–25.

————. *A Primer of Infant Development*. San Francisco: W. H. Freeman, 1977.

Bowlby, John. *Attachment and Loss*. Vol. 1: *Attachment*. 2nd ed. New York: Basic Books, 1983.

————. *Attachment and Loss*. Vol. 2: *Separation*. New York: Basic Books, 1973.

————. *Attachment and Loss*. Vol 3: *Loss*. New York: Basic Books, 1972.

————. *Can I Leave My Baby?* London: National Association for Mental Health, 1958.

————. *Child Care and the Growth of Love*. Harmondsworth: Penguin, 1953.

————. "Childhood Origins of Recidivism." *Howard Journal* 7 (1) (1945): 30–33.

————. *Forty-four Juvenile Thieves: Their Characters and Home-life*. London: Ballière, Tindall & Cox, 1946.

Bowlby, John, Karl Figlio, and Robert M. Young. "An Interview With John Bowlby on the Origins and Reception of His Work." *Free Associations* 6 (1986): 36–64.

————. *The Making and Breaking of Affectional Bonds*. New York: Methuen, 1979.

————. *Maternal Care and Mental Health*. 2nd ed. Albany: World Health Organization, 1952.

———— "A Note on Mother-Child Separation As a Mental Health Hazard." *British Journal of Medical Psychology* 31 (3) (1958): 247–48.

————. "Perspective: A Contribution by John Bowlby." *Bulletin of the Royal College of Psychiatrists* 5 (1) (1981): 1.

————. "The Rediscovery of the Family." In *Rediscovery of the Family*. See Bowlby et al., eds., 1981: 1–7.

————. "The Relation Between the Therapeutic Approach and the Legal Approach to Juvenile Delinquency." *Magistrate* 8 (1949): 260–64.

Bowlby, John, and James Robertson. "Responses of Young Children to Separation from Their Mothers." *Courrier of the International Children's Center,* Paris, Vol. 2 (2) (1962): 131–140.

Bowlby, John. *The Roots of Parenthood.* London: The National Children's Home, 1953.

Bowlby, John, James Robertson, and Dina Rosenbluth. "A Two-Year-Old Goes to Hospital." *The Psychoanalytic Study of the Child* Vol. 7 (1952): 82–94.

Bowlby, John. "Why Delinquency? The Case for Operational Research." Report of a Conference on the Scientific Study of Juvenile Delinquency. London: 1949.

Bowlby, John et al., eds. *Rediscovery of the Family.* Aberdeen: Aberdeen University Press, 1981.

Branthwaite, Alan, and Don Rogers, eds. *Children Growing Up.* New York: Taylor & Francis, 1985.

Bretherton, Inge. "Attachment Theory: Retrospect and Prospect." *In Growing Points of Attachment Theory and Research.* See Bretherton and Waters, eds., 1986: 3–38.

Bretherton, Inge, and Everett Waters, eds. "Growing Points of Attachment Theory and Research." *Monographs of the Society for Research in Child Development* 50 (1–2), 1986.

Bronfenbrenner, Urie. *Two Worlds of Childhood.* London: George Allen and Unwin, 1971.

Brophy, Beth, and Maureen Walsh. "Children Under Stress." *U.S. News and World Report* (October 27, 1986): 58–63.

Brown, George, and Tirril Harris. *Social Origins of Depression.* New York: Free Press, 1978.

Browne, Naima. "Do the Gentlemen in Whitehall Know Best? An Historical Perspective of Pre-School Provision in Britain." In *Untying the Apron Strings.* See Browne and France, eds., 1986: 8–31.

Browne, Naima, and Pauline France, eds. *Untying the Apron Strings.* Milton Keynes: Open University Press, 1986.

Bruner, Jerome. *The Relevance of Education.* New York: Norton, 1971.

————. *Under Five in Britain.* London: Grant McIntyre, 1980.

Burgoyne, Jacqueline, Roger Ormrod, and Martin Richards. *Divorce Matters.* Harmondsworth: Penguin, 1987.

Burgoyne, Jacqueline. "Material Happiness." *New Society* (April 10, 1987): 12–14.

Busfield, Joan, and Michael Paddon. *Thinking About Children*. New York: Cambridge University Press, 1977.

Carpenter, Genevieve. "Mother's Face and the Newborn." In *Child Alive*. See Lewin, ed., 1975: 126–36.

Chesler, Phyllis. *Mothers on Trial*. New York: McGraw Hill, 1986.

Chodorow, Nancy. *The Reproduction of Mothering*. Berkeley: University of California Press, 1978.

CIBA Foundation Symposium 33. *Parent-Infant Interaction*. Amsterdam: Elsevier, 1975.

Clarke, Ann M., and A. D. B. Clarke. *Early Experience: Myth and Evidence*. London: Open Books, 1976.

Clarke-Stewart, Alison. *Day Care*. The Developing Child Series. Cambridge: Harvard University Press, 1982.

Cohen, Bronwen, and Karen Clarke, eds. *Childcare and Equal Opportunities: Some Policy Perspectives*. London: HMSO/EOC, 1986.

Corter, Carl. "Infant Attachments." In *New Perspectives in Child Development*. See Foss, ed., 1974: 164–83.

Dally, Ann. *Inventing Motherhood*. New York: Schocken, 1983.

de Courcy Hinds, M. "They Fell in Love at First Sight." *New York Times* (February 14, 1981): 13–15.

Delozier, Pauline P. "Attachment Theory and Child Abuse." In *The Place of Attachment in Human Behavior*. See Parkes and Stevenson-Hinde, eds. (1982): 95–117.

de Mause, Lloyd. "The Evolution of Childhood." In *The History of Childhood*. See de Mause, ed., 1974: 1–74.

———, ed. *The History of Childhood*. New York: Psychohistory Press, 1974.

Denzin, Norman K. *Childhood Socialization*. San Francisco: Jossey-Bass, 1977.

de Unamuno, Miguel. *The Tragic Sense of Life*. Princeton: Princeton University Press, 1921.

Dingwall, Robert, John Eekelaar, and Topsy Murray. *The Protection of Children*. New York: Basil Blackwell, 1985.

Dowrick, Stephanie, and Sibyl Grundberg. "Introduction." In *Why Children?* See Dowrick and Grundberg, eds., 1980: 7–14.

———, eds. *Why Children?* San Diego: Harcourt Brace Jovanovich, 1981.

Dunn, Judy. *Distress and Comfort*. The Developing Child Series. Cambridge: Harvard University Press, 1977.

Dunn, Judy, and Carol Kendrick. *Siblings*. Cambridge: Harvard University Press, 1982.

Dunn, Judy. *Sisters and Brothers.* The Developing Child Series. Cambridge: Harvard University Press, 1985.

Eichenbaum, Luise, and Susie Orbach. *What Do Women Want?* New York: Putnam Publishing Group, 1983.

Eisenstein, Hester. *Contemporary Feminist Thought.* Boston: G. K. Hall, 1984.

Ennew, Judith. *The Sexual Exploitation of Children.* New York: St. Martin's Press, 1986.

Erikson, Erik. *Childhood and Society,* 2nd ed. New York: Norton, 1964.

Fisher, Seymour, and Roger P. Greenberg. *The Scientific Credibility of Freud's Theories and Therapy.* New York: Columbia University Press, 1985.

Fontana, Vincent J. *Somewhere a Child Is Crying.* New York: Mentor, 1973.

Foss, B., ed. *New Perspectives in Child Development.* Harmondsworth: Penguin, 1974.

Fox, Robin. *Encounter with Anthropology.* San Diego: Harcourt Brace Jovanovich, 1968.

Franklin, Bob. "Introduction." In *The Rights of Children.* See Franklin, ed., 1986: 1–23.

———, ed. *The Rights of Children.* New York: Basil Blackwell, 1986.

Freeman, Derek. *Margaret Mead and Samoa.* Cambridge: Harvard University Press, 1983.

Freeman, M. D. A. *The Rights and Wrongs of Children.* Wolfeboro, N.H.: Longwood Publishing Group, 1983.

Freud, Anna, and Sophie Dann. "An Experiment in Group Upbringing." *Psychoanalytic Study of the Child* Vol. 6 (1951): 127–68.

Friday, Nancy. *My Mother My Self.* New York: Dell, 1977.

Friedan, Betty. *The Feminine Mystique.* New York: Norton, 1963.

———. *The Second Stage.* New York: Summit Books, 1981.

Fromm, Erich. *The Art of Loving.* New York: Harper & Row, 1956.

Gathorne-Hardy, Jonathan. *The Rise and Fall of the British Nanny.* London: Hodder & Stoughton, 1972.

Gilligan, Carol. *In a Different Voice.* Cambridge: Harvard University Press, 1982.

Gordon, Linda. "Feminism and Social Control: The Case of Child Abuse and Neglect." In *What Is Feminism?* See Mitchell and Oakley, eds., 1986: 63–84.

Graham, Helen. "Maternal Deprivation." In *Children Growing Up.* See Branthwaite and Rogers, eds., 1985: 17–25.

Greer, Germaine. *Sex and Destiny.* New York: Harper & Row, 1985.

Gruber, Howard E. *Darwin on Man.* New York: E. P. Dutton, 1974.

Hall, David, and Margaret Stacy, eds. *Beyond Separation.* London: Routledge and Kegan Paul, 1979.

Hardyment, Christina. *Dream Babies.* Oxford: Oxford University Press, 1984.

Herbert, Martin. *Caring for Your Children.* New York, Basil Blackwell, 1985.

Hergenhahn, B. R. *An Introduction to Theories of Learning.* Englewood Cliffs, N.J.: Prentice-Hall, 1976.

Hewlett, Sylvia Ann. *A Lesser Life: The Myth of Women's Liberation.* New York: Warner, 1987.

Hinde, Robert A. *Ethology.* New York: Oxford University Press, 1982.

————. "Mothers' and Infants' Roles: Distinguishing the Questions to Be Asked." In *Parent-Infant Interaction.* See CIBA. 1975: 5–16.

Hiner, N. Ray, and Joseph M. Hawes. "Introduction." In *Growing Up in America.* See Hiner and Hawes, eds. 1985: xiii–xxv.

————, ed. *Growing Up in America.* Urbana: University of Illinois Press, 1985.

Hubbard, Ruth. "Personal Courage Is Not Enough: Some Hazards of Child-bearing in the 1980s." In *Test-Tube Women.* See Arditti, Klein, and Minden, eds., 1984: 331–55.

Hutter, Bridget, and Gillian Williams, eds. *Controlling Women.* New York: Methuen, 1981.

Immelmann, K., G. W. Barlow, L. Petrinovich, and M. Main, eds. *Behavioral Development.* New York: Cambridge University Press, 1981.

Ingleby, David. "Development in Social Context." In *Children of Social Worlds.* See Richards and Light, eds., 1986: 297–317.

Kaye, Kenneth. *The Mental and Social Life of Babies.* Chicago: University of Chicago Press, 1982.

Kitzinger, Sheila. *Women As Mothers.* New York: Random House, 1979.

————. "Women's Experiences of Birth at Home." In *The Place of Birth.* See Kitzinger and Davis, eds., 1978: 135–56.

Kitzinger, Sheila, and John A. Davis. *The Place of Birth.* New York: Oxford University Press, 1978.

Klaus, Marshall H., and John H. Kennell. "Maternal-Infant Bonding." In *Maternal-Infant Bonding.* See Klaus and Kennell, eds., 1976.

————, eds. *Maternal-Infant Bonding.* St. Louis: C. V. Mosby, 1976.

Kuper, Adam. "Plus ça Change." *New Society* (March 20, 1987): 29–30.

Laing, R. D. *The Politics of Experience.* Harmondsworth: Penguin, 1967.

————. *The Politics of the Family and Other Essays*. New York: Random House, 1972.

Lamm, Maurice. *The Jewish Way in Love and Marriage*. San Francisco: Harper & Row, 1980.

Lane, Robert E. "Waiting for Lefty: The Capitalist Genesis of Socialist Man." *Theory and Society* 6 (1978): 1–28.

Lasch, Christopher. *The Minimal Self*. New York: Norton, 1984.

Laslett, Peter. *Family Life and Illicit Love in Earlier Generations*. New York: Cambridge University Press, 1977.

Lee, Constance M., ed. *Child Abuse*. Milton Keynes: Open University Press, 1978.

Leiderman, P. "Human Mother-Infant Social Bonding: Is There a Sensitive Period?" In *Behavioral Development*. See Immelmann, Barlow, Petrinovich, and Main, eds., 1981: 14–28.

Lewin, Roger, ed. *Child Alive*. London: Temple Smith, 1975.

Lewis, Charles. *Becoming a Father*. New York: Taylor & Francis, 1986.

Lewis, Michael, and Leonard A. Rosenblum, eds. *The Effect of the Infant on Its Caregiver*. New York: John Wiley, 1974.

Liedloff, Jean, *The Continuum Concept*. Reading, Mass.: Addison-Wesley, 1975.

Lomax, Elizabeth M. R. *Science and Patterns of Child Care*. San Francisco: W. H. Freeman, 1978.

Lorenz, K. "Der Kumpan in der Umwelt des Vogels." *J. F. Ornith* 83 (1935): 137–213.

McConville, Brigid. *Sisters: Love and Conflict within the Lifelong Bond*. London: Pan, 1985.

Mead, Margaret. *Coming of Age in Samoa*. Magnolia, Mass.: Peter Smith, 1928.

Mitchell, Ann. *Children in the Middle*. New York: Methuen, 1985.

Mitchell, Juliet, and Ann Oakley, eds. *What Is Feminism?* New York: Pantheon, 1986.

Moskovitz, Sarah. "Longitudinal Follow-up of Child Survivors of the Holocaust." *Journal of the American Academy of Child Psychiatry* 24 (4) (1985): 401–7.

Moss, Peter. "Some Principles for a Childcare Service for Working Parents." In *Childcare and Equal Opportunities*. See Cohen and Clarke, eds., 1986: 19–34.

Murchison, C., ed. *Psychologists of 1925*. Worcester, Mass.: Clark University Press, 1926.

New, Caroline, and Miriam David. *For the Children's Sake.* New York: Penguin, 1986.

Newson, John, and Elizabeth Newson. *Patterns of Infant Care.* Harmondsworth: Penguin, 1965.

Oakley, Ann. "Feminism and Motherhood." In *Children of Social Worlds.* See Richards and Light, eds., 1986: 74–94.

————. *From Here to Maternity.* Harmondsworth: Penguin, 1986.

————. "Normal Motherhood: An Exercise in Self Control." In *Controlling Women.* See Hutter and Williams, eds., 1981: 79–107.

————. *The Sociology of Housework.* New York: Pantheon, 1975.

————. *Subject Women.* New York: Pantheon, 1981.

————. *Telling the Truth About Jerusalem.* New York: Basil Blackwell, 1986.

Packard, Vance. *A Nation of Strangers.* London: McKay, 1972.

Packman, Jean. *Who Needs Care?* New York: Basil Blackwell, 1986.

Parke, Ross D. *Fathers.* The Developing Child Series. Cambridge: Harvard University Press, 1981.

Parkes, Colin Murray. *Bereavement.* Madison, Conn.: International Universities Press, 1973.

Parkes, Colin Murray, and Robert S. Weiss. *Recovery from Bereavement.* New York: Basic Books, 1983.

Parkes, Colin Murray, and Joan Stevenson-Hinde, eds. *The Place of Attachment in Human Behavior.* New York: Basic Books, 1982.

Penfold, P. Susan, and Gillian A. Walker. *Women and the Psychiatric Paradox.* Montreal: Eden Press, 1983.

Plath, Sylvia. *The Journals of Sylvia Plath.* New York: Doubleday, 1982.

Pollock, Linda A. *Forgotten Children: Parent-Child Relations from 1500–1900.* New York: Cambridge University Press, 1984.

Pound, Andrea. "Attachment and Maternal Depression." In *The Place of Attachment in Human Behavior.* See Parkes and Stevenson-Hinde, eds., 1982: 118–30.

Pringle, Mia Kellmer. "The Needs of Children." In *Child Abuse.* See Lee, ed., 1978: 26–31.

Ribble, Margaret. *The Rights of Infants.* New York: Columbia University Press, 1943.

Rich, Adrienne. *Of Women Born.* New York: Norton, 1976.

Richards, M. P. M. "Early Separation." In *Child Alive.* See Lewin, ed., 1975: 23–31.

————. "Non-Accidental Injury to Children in an Ecological Perspective." DHSS Conference Paper, June 1974.

Richards, M. P. M., and Paul Light, eds. *Children of Social Worlds*. Oxford: Polity Press, 1986.

Richards, M. P. M., ed. *The Integration of a Child into a Social World*. New York: Cambridge University Press, 1974.

Ricks, Margaret H. "The Social Transmission of Parental Behavior: Attachment Across Generations." In *Growing Points of Attachment Theory and Research*. See Bretherton and Waters, eds., 1986: 211–27.

Riley, Denise. *War in the Nursery*. Topsfield, Mass.: Salem House, 1984.

Robertson, James, ed. *Hospitals and Children: A Parent's-Eye View*. Madison, Conn.: International Universities Press, 1963.

Robertson, James, and Joyce Robertson. "The Importance of Substitute Mothering for the Long-stay Child." *Health and Social Service Journal* (April 20, 1974): 7.

———. *Young Children in Brief Separation: A Fresh Look*. New York: Quadrangle Books, 1971.

Rowland, Robyn. "Reproductive Technologies: The Final Solution to the Women Question?" In *Test-Tube Women*. See Arditti, Klein, and Minden, eds., 1984: 356–69.

Rubin, Zick. *Children's Friendships*. Cambridge: Harvard University Press, 1980.

Rutter, Michael. *Maternal Deprivation Reassessed*. Harmondsworth: Penguin, 1972.

Rycroft, Charles. *Psychoanalysis and Beyond*. Chicago: University of Chicago Press, 1986.

Scarf, Maggie. *Unfinished Business*. New York: Doubleday, 1980.

Schaffer, H. Rudolph. *The Child's Entry into a Social World*. San Diego: Academic Press, 1984.

Schaffer, H. Rudolph, and Peggy E. Emerson. "The Development of Social Attachments in Infancy." *Monographs of the Society for Research in Child Development* 29 (3) (1964): 3–76.

Schaffer, H. R. "Early Interactive Development." In *Studies in Mother-Infant Interaction*. See Schaffer, ed., 1977: 3–18.

Schaffer, Rudolph. *Mothering*. Cambridge: Harvard University Press, 1977.

Schaffer, H. R., ed. *Studies in Mother-Infant Interaction*. San Diego: Academic Press, 1977.

Segal, Lynne. "Women's Retreat into Motherhood." *New Statesman* (January 1, 1987): 16–18.

Sharpe, Sue. *Double Identity: The Lives of Working Mothers*. Harmondsworth: Penguin, 1984.

Shaw, Nancy Stoller. *Forced Labor: Maternity Care in the United States.* New York: Pergamon, 1974.

Shorter, Edward. *A History of Women's Bodies.* Harmondsworth: Penguin, 1984.

Sluckin, Wladyslaw, Martin Herbert, and Alice Sluckin. *Maternal Bonding.* New York: Basil Blackwell, 1984.

Sluckin, Wladyslaw, and Martin Herbert, eds. *Parental Behavior.* New York: Basil Blackwell, 1986.

Smith, F. V. *Attachment of the Young.* Edinburgh: Oliver and Boyd, 1969.

Sorel, Nancy Caldwell. *Ever Since Eve.* New York: Oxford University Press, 1984.

Spitz, R. A., and K. M. Wolf. "Anaclitic Depression: An Inquiry into the Genesis of Psychiatric Conditions in Early Childhood." *The Psychoanalytic Study of the Child,* Vol. 2 (1946): 113–17.

Spock, Benjamin. *Baby and Child Care.* New York: E. P. Dutton, 1945.

Steedman, Carolyn, Cathy Urwin, and Valerie Walkerdine, eds. *Language, Gender and Childhood.* New York: Methuen, 1985.

Stein, Mike, and Kate Carey. *Leaving Care.* New York: Basil Blackwell, 1986.

Suomi, Stephen J. et al. "Effects of Maternal and Peer Separations on Young Monkeys." *Journal of Child Psychology and Psychiatry* 17 (1976): 101–12.

Sylva, Kathy, and Ingrid Lunt. *Child Development: A First Course.* Oxford: Basil Blackwell, 1982.

Thoburn, June, Anne Murdoch, and Alison O'Brien. *Permanence in Child Care.* New York: Basil Blackwell, 1987.

Tivers, Jacqueline. *Women Attached.* Wellesley, Mass.: St. Martin, 1985.

Tizard, Barbara. "The Care of Young Children." *Thomas Coram Research Unit Working and Occasional Papers.* London: University of London Institute of Education, 1986.

Tizard, Jack. "Psychology and Social Policy." *Bulletin of British Psychological Society* 29 (1976): 225–34.

Tizard, Jack, and Barbara Tizard. "The Institution as an Environment for Development." In *The Integration of a Child into a Social World.* See Richards, ed. (1974): 137–52.

Toynbee, Polly. *Lost Children: The Story of Adopted Children Searching for Their Mothers.* London: Coronet, 1987.

Trowell, Judith. "Effects of Obstetric Management on the Mother-Child Relationship." In *The Place of Attachment in Human Behavior.* See Parkes and Stevenson-Hinde, eds., 1982: 79–94.

UNICEF Staff, and James P. Grant, eds. *The State of the World's Children*. New York: Oxford University Press, 1983.

Urwin, Cathy. "Constructing Motherhood: The Persuasion of Normal Development." In *Language, Gender and Childhood*. See Steedman, Urwin, and Walkerdine, eds., 1985: 164–202.

Valentine, Charles A. *Culture and Poverty*. Chicago: University of Chicago Press, 1968.

Wakerman, Elyce. *Father Loss*. New York: Doubleday, 1984.

Wallerstein, Judith S., and Joan B. Kelly. *Surviving the Breakup*. New York: Basic Books, 1982.

Watson, J. B. "Experimental Studies on the Growth of Emotions." In *Psychologists of 1925*. See Murchison, ed., 1926: 10–28.

———. *Psychological Care of the Infant and Child.* Salem, N.H.: Ayer, 1928.

Weiss, Nancy Pottishman. "Mother, the Invention of Necessity: Dr. Benjamin Spock's 'Baby and Child Care.'" In *Growing Up in America*. See Hiner and Hawes, eds., 1985: 283–303.

Wilson, Elizabeth. *Only Halfway to Paradise*. New York: Methuen, 1980.

Winnicott, D. W. *The Child, the Family, and the Outside World*. Harmondsworth: Penguin, 1964.

———. *Home Is Where We Start From*. New York: Norton, 1986.

Yankelovich, Daniel. *New Rules: Searching for Self-Fulfillment in a World Turned Upside Down*. New York: Random House, 1981.

Young, Michael, and Peter Willmott. *Family and Kinship in East London*. New York: Penguin, 1963.

Zelizer, Viviana A. *Pricing the Priceless Child*. New York: Basic Books, 1985.

Index

About the Author

BOB MULLAN was educated at the University of Newcastle upon Tyne (B.A.) and the London School of Economics and Political Science (Ph.D.). He taught sociology and psychology at the University of East Anglia, England, from 1978 to 1986 and now devotes his time to writing, producing television programs, and to a daily radio show for the BBC. He is the author of ten books and co-author of *Uninvited Guests*.